CAMBRIDGE LIBRARY COLLECTION

Books of enduring scholarly value

Polar Exploration

This series includes accounts, by eye-witnesses and contemporaries, of early expeditions to the Arctic and the Antarctic. Huge resources were invested in such endeavours, particularly the search for the North-West Passage, which, if successful, promised enormous strategic and commercial rewards. Cartographers and scientists travelled with many of the expeditions, and their work made important contributions to earth sciences, climatology, botany and zoology. They also brought back anthropological information about the indigenous peoples of the Arctic region and the southern fringes of the American continent. The series further includes dramatic and poignant accounts of the harsh realities of working in extreme conditions and utter isolation in bygone centuries.

The Impracticability of a North-West Passage for Ships, Impartially Considered

Peter Heywood (1772–1831) became known for his involvement in the 1789 mutiny aboard the *Bounty*. After evading a death sentence thanks to a royal pardon, he was able to advance himself in a distinguished naval career, achieving the rank of post-captain. The question of the North-West Passage, a sea route through the Arctic that would connect the Atlantic and Pacific oceans, remained an obsession for the British for much of the nineteenth century. Drawing on his experience as a naval hydrographer and writing under the pseudonym 'Scrutator', Heywood considers the question of the North-West Passage in this 1824 publication by surveying accounts of recent expeditions to the Arctic. While he does not dispute the existence of the much-sought route, he argues that the icy waters would not be navigable for ships. It was not until the early twentieth century that Roald Amundsen and his crew achieved the seemingly impossible.

T0382030

Cambridge University Press has long been a pioneer in the reissuing of out-of-print titles from its own backlist, producing digital reprints of books that are still sought after by scholars and students but could not be reprinted economically using traditional technology. The Cambridge Library Collection extends this activity to a wider range of books which are still of importance to researchers and professionals, either for the source material they contain, or as landmarks in the history of their academic discipline.

Drawing from the world-renowned collections in the Cambridge University Library and other partner libraries, and guided by the advice of experts in each subject area, Cambridge University Press is using state-of-the-art scanning machines in its own Printing House to capture the content of each book selected for inclusion. The files are processed to give a consistently clear, crisp image, and the books finished to the high quality standard for which the Press is recognised around the world. The latest print-on-demand technology ensures that the books will remain available indefinitely, and that orders for single or multiple copies can quickly be supplied.

The Cambridge Library Collection brings back to life books of enduring scholarly value (including out-of-copyright works originally issued by other publishers) across a wide range of disciplines in the humanities and social sciences and in science and technology.

The Impracticability of a North-West Passage for Ships,

Impartially Considered

Peter Heywood

CAMBRIDGE
UNIVERSITY PRESS

CAMBRIDGE
UNIVERSITY PRESS

University Printing House, Cambridge, CB2 8BS, United Kingdom

Cambridge University Press is part of the University of Cambridge.

It furthers the University's mission by disseminating knowledge in the pursuit of education, learning and research at the highest international levels of excellence.

www.cambridge.org
Information on this title: www.cambridge.org/9781108071864

This edition first published 1824
This digitally printed version 2014

ISBN 978-1-108-07186-4 Paperback

THE

IMPRACTICABILITY

OF

A NORTH-WEST PASSAGE

FOR

SHIPS,

IMPARTIALLY CONSIDERED.

———————————

LONDON:

1824.

PREFACE.

BEING what is termed " a sea-faring man," I am frequently asked questions concerning the North-West Passage, which, perhaps, would puzzle much wiser heads to answer; I have therefore been induced to read a little of what has been published on the subject, especially within the last seven or eight years, by those, who are supposed to have considered it most, or have detailed the results of their experience in the Arctic regions.

I was the more disposed to amuse myself in this way, from a desire to judge for myself if possible, why all former adventurers, as well as Captains Ross, Buchan, and Parry, have failed in an enterprise, which the Quarterly Review has represented as " of no difficult execution," and merely " the business of three months out and home;" and also from seeing it mentioned in the public papers that another attempt is to be made this year, by Captains Parry and Hoppner, in the Fury and Hecla, by way of Lancaster Sound, and

Prince Regent's Inlet, along the northern shores of America.

Without pretending to give any decided opinion of my own, on this "interesting question," I am free to say, that the facts stated, and (of course) believed by the authors from whom I have quoted, and who have advocated the practicability as well as the existence of a North-West passage, appear to me to show its impracticability for ships, even *if* there *be* one for water and fish (for the river Thames, if frozen over, would still be a river, but *unnavigable*), and to render its very existence more doubtful than ever.

Whether, or not, the inferences I have drawn from the DATA furnished chiefly, if not entirely, by those advocates themselves, be fair and legitimate, I leave to the decision of those unbiassed (particularly nautical) readers, who are most competent to form a correct judgment on and disposed to give their attention to such a subject.

SCRUTATOR.

[*London, 25th March,* 1824.

" A PLAIN MATTER-OF-FACT MAN WISHES FOR DATA
RATHER THAN WILD HYPOTHESES."

Quart. Rev. xxviii. 398.

AFTER a lapse of about twenty-six years, the question of the Existence, as well as the *Practicability*, of a Passage for ships, from the Atlantic to the Pacific, was revived ; and the attention of the public excited in the year 1817, by the writer of an article headed " Lord Selkirk, and the North-West Passage," in No. 31. of " a popular critical Journal." Having introduced the latter subject by an examination into the authenticity of " Voyage de la Mer Glaciale ; par le Capitaine Laurent Ferrer Maldonado, l'an 1588," the Reviewer says, " Destitute as we consider the relation of Maldonado to be, both of veracity and authenticity, we are by no means inclined to suppose that such a voyage, as it describes, is *impracticable. We firmly believe,* on the contrary, that *a navigable passage does exist,* and may be of *no difficult* execution. Why then, it may be asked, have all the attempts made at different times, from both sides the continent of America, failed ?—Because, not one of them was ever made near that part of the coast of America round which, it is most likely, the passage would lead into the Frozen or Northern Ocean. The distance between *Baffin's Sea* and Behring's Strait, is not

Data.   **A**

more than 1200 miles. Could we only be certain that Hearne and Mackenzie actually arrived at the shore of the Northern Ocean, the *existence* of a passage would amount nearly to a certainty. The solution of this important problem is the business of three months out and home. The space to be examined, at the *very utmost*, is from the 67th to the 71st parallels, or 4° of latitude ! ! If the continent of America shall be found to terminate, as is most likely, about the 70° of latitude, or even below it, we have little doubt of a *free* and *practicable passage round it, for seven or eight months* in every year; and we are much mistaken if the North-west Company would not derive immediate and incalculable advantages from a passage of *three months* to their establishments on Columbia river, instead of the circuitous voyage of six or seven months round Cape Horn; to say nothing of the benefit which might be derived from taking their cargoes of furs and peltry for the China market at Mackenzie's and Copper-mine rivers, to which the northern Indians would be *too happy* to bring them, if protected by European establishments at these, or other places, from their enemies the Esquimaux."

What flattering prospects are here held forth to the North-west Company of " incalculable advantages," and to the " northern Indians" of being made even " too happy ! !" Nothing like a fear is expressed, of obstacles to be met with and surmounted. On the contrary, all is *plain sailing* through " a free and *practicable passage* for seven or eight months in every year." The language of the foregoing extracts is calculated to raise, not only the hopes, but the expectations of the public, as high as those which the writer himself no doubt indulged in, as to the success of any future attempt; provided it should be made where he recommends, *near the north-east part of America.* He seems, however, to have been aware of there being some little difficulty in getting hold of that part of America, for he informs us a little further on, at page 169, that, "Hitherto, most of our adventurers have worked their way through Hudson's Strait, which is generally choked up with ice, then standing *to the northward*, they have had to contend with ice drifting to the southward, with contrary winds and currents. These inconveniences," he adds, "would be obviated by standing *first* to the latitudes of 71° or 72°, and from thence southerly and westerly, till they saw the north-east coast of America, which would go far to complete the discovery, or, till they reached Hudson's Bay, which would *decide* the question in the *negative.*" Here, in the most direct terms, this reviewer records *his disapprobation* (and with good reason) of a route through Hudson's Strait and Bay, in quest of the north-east part of America ; nay *his belief,* at the time he wrote, that No passage could be found out of Hudson's Bay, (and consequently even through the Welcome or *Repulse* Bay) into the Polar sea. Inasmuch as he says, that if the more northerly route he recommends, should (by a southerly and westerly deviation afterwards) lead any future adventurer *into Hudson's Bay, That* " would *decide* the question in the *negative."* And yet in the same article, at page 162, this reviewer would seem to doubt the veracity of Middleton ; " who," he informs us, "looked into (he says, sailed round,) what he (Middleton) was pleased to call *Repulse Bay."* It is indeed very amusing to compare some of the notions of this anonymous writer, in different numbers of this " popular critical journal," on points connected with the question of a north-west passage. For instance, in this Number 31, at page 170 ; he says—" It is a common, but we believe an erroneous opinion, that the temperature of our climate has regularly been diminishing, and that it is owing to the ice having permanently fixed itself to the shores of Greenland, which in consequence, from being once a flourishing colony of Denmark, is now become uninhabitable and unapproachable. We *doubt* both the *fact* and the *inference.* *It is not the climate that has altered,* but *we* who feel it more severe as we advance in years; the registers of the absolute degree of temperature, as measured by the thermometer, do not warrant any *such conclusion ;* and more attempts than one to land on the coast of Greenland must be made, before we can give credit to its being bound up in eternal ice—which is known to shift about with every gale of wind, to be drifted by currents, and to crumble and consume *below the surface of the water.*"

Now, this is all very probable, and perhaps would not have been questioned by any body, but the reviewer himself. He, however, having a favourite hypothesis to maintain, which he seems to have founded on *imaginary assumptions,* at variance with each other, rather than on known facts and experience, tells us quite a different thing in No. 35, of the Quarterly Review, in an article written preparatory to the fitting out of the two expeditions in the beginning of the following year 1818; as it was very necessary to clear away (at least by *pen and ink)* as much as possible of the ice, which some ignorant folks might suppose would otherwise impede their progress through the Polar regions, towards Behring's Strait; he therefore *admits,* in the first place, " that, for the last four hundred years, an extensive portion of the eastern coast of Old Greenland *has* been shut up, by an *impenetrable* barrier of ice, and with it the ill-fated Norwegian or Danish colonies; and who were thus cut off at once from all communication with the mother-country ;"—that " various attempts have been made, from time to time, to approach this coast, but *in vain;* the ice being every where impervious ; and that all *hope* being at length abandoned, that part of this extensive tract of land, which faces the east, took the appropriate name of *lost* Greenland. The event to which we have alluded is the disappearance of the whole, or greater part of this barrier of ice. How the Danes can now pretend to *doubt,* as one of their writers affects to do, whether there *ever were a colony* on the *eastern* side is, *to us,* quite *inexplicable,* unless it be to palliate their negligence at the first approach of the ice, and their want of humanity since." In short, the reviewer has, *now, no doubt* of this extraordinary fact, for nothing could have happened so opportunely ; and he therefore adduces the authority of many persons in various places to *prove it,* and even assigns as " the most probable cause, for the *sudden* departure of all this ice, its having broken loose by its own weight ! !" Having thus " established beyond any doubt, the fact of the disappearance of the ice," he asks, whether any, and what advantages may arise out of an event which, for the first time has occurred, at least to so great an extent, during the last four hundred years ? and answers, first, The *influence* which the removal of so large a body of ice may have on our own climate.

2ndly. The opportunity it affords of enquiring into the fate of the *long-lost colony* on the eastern coast of Old Greenland.

3rdly. The *facility* it offers, of correcting the very defective geography of the Arctic regions in our western hemisphere, and of attempting the circumnavigation of Old Greenland, a direct passage over the Pole, and the more circuitous one along the northern coast of America into the Pacific. He then takes pains *to prove deterioration of climate to have taken place* in Iceland, Switzerland and Pennsylvania, and that " it must be equally clear therefore, that *our own climate*, though in a less degree, *must have been affected* by this vast accumulation of Ice on the coast of Greenland :" and gives " reasons for believing, that previously to the fifteenth century England enjoyed a *warmer summer climate than since that period ! !*"

The reviewer having, as we have seen in a former number, expressed his belief of the *practicability*, as well as the existence, of a passage for ships from the Atlantic to the Pacific through Behring's Strait ; he proceeds to explain his grounds for that belief.

1st. He asserts the existence of " a perpetual current setting down from the northward, (sometimes with a velocity of four or even five miles an hour) along the eastern coast of America and the western shores of Old Greenland ;" and thereon *assumes* " an uninterrupted communication, between Davis Strait and the Great Polar Basin," the consequent insularity of Old Greenland, and the non-existence of Baffin's Bay.

2ndly, That vast quantities of drift wood were floated down by this current from the northward, consisting of trees the produce of Asia and America (some, perhaps, through Behring's Strait), by means of *his* " circum- volving current," between the Pacific and the Atlantic, " round the north coast of America." As these grounds were not satisfactory, and much other matter contained in this article appeared rather visionary, and calculated to raise the public expectation of success too high, by annihilating probable, or at least possible difficulties, an anonymous writer was induced to publish a reply to it in the Naval Chronicle for the month of March, 1818, just before the expeditions sailed, under Captains Ross and Buchan. In extracting it here, I shall adduce such facts and experiments, made known to us by those who have since written on the subject, or visited the Arctic regions, as tend to prove, or disprove, the opinions of either of these writers.

The letter of Phoca, in the Naval Chronicle, is dated Hull, 27th Feb. 1818. I shall be excused for making copious extracts from it; particularly as it happened to be inserted in a work of very limited circulation at the time; and the correctness of many of his opinions has been practically proved, so far, by the failure of every expedition by sea, since he wrote this letter.

He says, " The appearance of an article in the Quarterly Review, for this month, on the subject of the expeditions, now fitting out, to explore the Arctic regions, has led me to consider some of the matters therein stated, and to enquire into the solidity of some of the writer's notions on this interesting topic." After a few preliminary observations on the fact of the late reported disappearance of ice, from the eastern coast of Old Greenland, and its supposed connexion with the phænomena of Magnetism, Electricity, and the Aurora Borealis, he proceeds : " The removal of this ice being ' cotemporaneous with the period when the western declination of the magnetic needle became stationary,' is certainly ' a remarkable coincidence.' At all events, in whatever way the supposed connexion may be, between the removal of the ice, and these phænomena, it seems not unfair to infer, that the departure of the immense *mountains* and fields of ice which for so many centuries have covered the Arctic seas, *may* have had some effect in stopping the career of the western declination of the needle." But we may *as fairly* draw the same inference from a similar cause, though probably of much less extent ; and all we *can* know, till the whole of the Arctic Regions is explored, viz. the departure of, perhaps, a *very small portion* only, of those " immense *mountains* and fields of ice, which had collected in the vicinity *of Greenland.* What may still remain in the Arctic seas, we are yet to learn ; and concerning which, like every thing else, where facts and local experience are wanting, our opinions can only be formed on fixed and received principles. The fact, however, of the disappearance of *some* large mountains and fields of ice from *part* of the Arctic regions, being *admitted,* the Quarterly Reviewer's enquiry as to its supposed influence on our climate, is thus treated : " On the benefits we should derive from an amelioration of our climate, there can be but one opinion. That our Summer seasons have been colder than usual, in the latter years, for instance, and from the causes he assigns, few will doubt. But the effect produced may not continue. For though the principal cause of the chilliness of our climate, compared with what it appears to have been centuries ago, may be removed *for the present,* yet, the grand primary cause which produced the ice, whose approximation deteriorated our climate, it is presumed will continue to operate ; and what has happened by the established general law of nature, may happen again. Therefore, though it may be *hoped,* it certainly would be " unreasonable to *presume,*" that, merely on account of the present accidental removal of *some portion* of ice, " our Summer climate (and Winter too, when the wind blows from the western quarter) may henceforth improve. Though no doubt it will improve, *if* the ice does not again collect in the place from whence it has lately been dislodged. But surely we have more *reason* to fear it *may*, because it *has* done so before, than to presume we shall 'henceforth' have no more huge icebergs drifting down to the southward in the wind's eye of our island, and that *therefore* our climate may improve. For whilst the universe continues to be governed by the unerring and unalterable laws of God, mountains and fields of ice will doubtless continue to be formed in the Polar regions of the north; and whenever the winters are successively severe there, they must accumulate, and no doubt find their way to the southward, as they have done.

" With respect to 'the opportunity which the *local* disappearance of the ice affords, of enquiring into the fate of the long lost colony, on the eastern coast of Old Greenland, it must be admitted to be favorable. And should the east coast of Greenland continue to be as free from ice as it is said to have been last year, it is probable the object may be attained.'—Great part of this coast has since been visited and laid down by Mr. Scoresby,' and also by Captain Sabine in His Majesty's ship Griper.

" The reviewer's third object is, 'the facility the removal of the ice offers, of correcting the very defective geography of the Arctic regions in our western hemisphere; of attempting the circumnavigation of Old Greenland—a direct passage over the Pole—and the more circuitous one along the northern coast of America, into the Pacific.' Certainly, 'any event that tends to encourage the attempt to amend the very defective

' Mr. Scoresby has published an account of his observations on this coast; which has also since been visited by Captain Sabine in His Majesty's ship the Griper.

Data. B

geography of the Arctic regions, more especially on the side of America, may be hailed as an important occur‑ rence.' But let us see whether what may be *only* a *local*, and very *partial*, removal of ice collected in the vicinity of Greenland, is likely to facilitate more, than an examination of its eastern coast, or at most its cir‑ cumnavig ation; and perhaps, of exploring the coast of America, some distance to the north-west of Cum‑ berland Island, if not to its north-east extremity. It is very true that several circumstances may be adduced in support of the opinion, that Greenland is either an island, or an archipelago of islands, and none stronger than the ' perpetual current *stated* to set down to the southward along the eastern coast of America, and the western shores of Greenland.'

" But this current, though affording ' a strong pre‑ sumption' that 'between Davis' Straits and the great Polar basin,' there *is some* communication, surely it does not authorise us to presume, that there *is* an ' *uninterrupted communication.*' On the contrary, it seems probable that there *must be islands* or shoals be‑ tween the north-west coast of Greenland and the north‑ east coast of America, among which small masses of ice, trees, and whales too, as well as current, *may* find passage down Davis' Straits from the ' Polar basin ;' but which may be, and probably *are, so blocked up*, gene‑ rally, by mountains and large fields of ice, as to present an *impassable* barrier *for Ships*. On account of this cur‑ rent (if it exist,) it is certainly fair to presume that the northern part of Davis' Straits is mis-named in the charts as ' a Bay ;' for, if it were one, ' it would be diffi‑ cult to explain how a current that runs to the southward perpetually (as we are told),' and sometimes with a velocity of four or five miles an hour, could originate in the bottom of it!"

I must observe here that the reviewer's head seems to have been so full of the *ideal* belief of an " *open sea* to the northward of Davis' Straits, and extending all the way to Behring's Straits, so as to allow of a communication, free and uninterrupted for ships between the Atlantic and Pacific," as well as for his imaginary circumvolving current, that he never once allowed *a fact* to enter, which would at once have destroyed that belief.—If he had examined the log-books of some of the Davis' Straits whale-ships, he would have discovered, that for days together, when laying to, under little or no canvas, their bearings of points on the west coast of Greenland, do not alter perhaps a point of the compass either way; and *therefore* that no such *extraordinary current* could possibly exist.[1] This simple fact must have struck Phoca's mind as a seaman at once; and though it seems to have made him sceptical, he does not venture to contradict the reviewer positively, but merely reserves himself for *further proof*, and pursues his subject with caution.— " *If*", says he, " *there is* ' an uninterrupted communication', that is, *if* there is no land, no shoals in the whole space between Greenland and America, it appears very probable that greater quantities of ice would pass through that space with a current of *such velocity*, and less find its way round Greenland.

" But we must first endeavor to decide, as well as we can, how, and where the ice in the Polar regions is formed; in what direction it is *probably* impelled by winds and currents; how these winds *probably*

---

[1] Its non-existence has been since proved by Captains Ross and Parry.

prevail in summer and winter ; and how the current *probably* sets *underneath* as well as at the surface of the water. For notwithstanding the writer of the article I am examining, apprehends ' it will be found that the currents of the ocean are entirely superficial, where no land intervenes ;' and though he says, ' it would be difficult to explain the perpetual egress of a current from the Polar basin into the Atlantic, without admitting a supply through the only remaining opening (Behring's Straits,) into that basin to supply the demand of the current,' I yet firmly believe that there must be a continual *underflow* of water in the ocean, as well as superficial currents ; otherwise ' that universal motion of the great deep' which he and all must allow, cannot satisfactorily be accounted for. How, then, it may be asked, are these lower currents to be accounted for ? The question is much easier to be put, than solved to the satisfaction of others. But I will endeavor to explain the ideas I have on the subject, as well as I can ; and that too with all the diffidence of one, who knows that though conjectures *may* perhaps be well founded, their truth depends on experiment.

" The conjectures I venture to offer are, however, founded on the known and acknowleged properties of Heat and cold. Heat is known to be the general cause of the expansion of air and water, and cold the cause of compression.—Heat rarefies, and cold condenses. The influence of the sun in rarefying the atmosphere to the greatest degree, between the tropics, together with the earth's rotation on its axis, from west to east, would produce a constant wind from east to west all round the globe, *if* no land intervened ; because, the points of greatest rarefaction being successively westward ; and those eastward of each other, parting successively, as the sun sets in their horizons, with part of the heat received in his passage over them, the motion of the atmosphere nearest the surface of the water must necessarily be from east to west, following the apparent motion of the sun. We find this proved by fact, on those portions of the globe where the general law is not obstructed by causes of an opposite nature, arising from terrene influence: viz., in the Pacific Ocean, between America and the east coast of New Holland, and also in the open sea between Africa and America. The central medium line of greatest rarefaction, is the equator; but according to the sun's declination north or south, it will be more to the northward or southward. The air thus rarefied in the lower regions of the atmosphere surrounding the earth, and comprised within the limits of the sun's path between the tropics, must be continually ascending into the higher, and thence, north of the equator, advancing towards the north pole; and south of the line, towards the south pole; till *somewhere*, in its passage, it acquires that degree of condensation by cold, which compels it again to return, in the lower strata, to the point of greatest rarefaction, to undergo the same process.

" This seems to be the grand general law of nature's operation on the atmosphere, that by ' universal motion, it may be preserved in a state of purity.' [1]

" Let us now enquire, whether this same law is not equally applicable to that universal motion of the great deep, which must be equally necessary to *its* purity, and which we may therefore certainly presume does

[1] This counter-flux from the equator to the poles, and *vice versa*, is demonstrated by Mr. Daniel in his Meteorological Essays, published in 1823, who explains why, " This interchange of the polar and equatorial atmospheres must tend to an equalisation of temperature."

take place on *some general* principle. We indeed already know, that the waters of the Pacific Ocean, and of the Atlantic, between the tropics, where least obstructed by land, move at and near the surface, in a similar direction, nearly and generally, to that of the wind.—When obstructed by lands, they take the various turnings and windings, which the forms and trendings of those lands, and other local causes, impose on them.

"If it be allowed, 'that the influence of the sun, in rarefying the atmosphere to the greatest degree, between the tropics, together with the earth's rotation on its axis from west to east, would produce (if no land intervened) a constant wind from east to west,' may we not suppose, if the same causes operate similarly, but proportionally, on the *waters* of the ocean, that *they* must produce a similar effect, and oblige them to take a like direction—that is, from east to west, at and near the surface all round the globe, within the limits of the sun's declination?—If this general effect, then, be admitted, on the ground it rests, we may presume, that if there were a passage through the Isthmus of Darien for the immense body of water, which continually flows from east to west into the Caribbean Sea and Gulf of Mexico, what is called the gulf-stream would no longer exist. And as it seems probable, that the surface of the water must be somewhat higher [1] on the eastern side of America *thereabouts*, than on the other, owing to the land's obstruction to the natural course of the great equinoctial current, and the necessity imposed

[1] From the observations made by Humboldt at the mouth of the Rio Seca in the Atlantic, and on the coast of the South Sea, it appears " there is a difference of level between the two seas, not exceeding 6 or 7 metres, or about 19 or 22 feet."

on it, to find vent through the Gulf of Florida, into the Atlantic ; it is not unreasonable to conclude, that if this accumulation of water was at liberty to flow through the Continent of America, into the Pacific Ocean, the surface of the sea, on this side (next the Atlantic) would be lower than it now is ; so that parts of land, now under water, would be exposed to view. This effect would, however, be injurious to commerce with the West Indies ; for it would render the homeward-bound passage more difficult. Instead of a constant weather current, to assist ships, it is pretty certain there would be a lee one from the north-east, along the east coast of Florida ; and its influence would most probably be felt, far up to the north-east ; from whence the current of colder water would flow, nearer the surface than it now can, covered superficially as it is by the warmer gulf-stream. The high degree of temperature which this great body of water acquires, by the sun's constant action upon it, being slowly reduced, during its propelled progress to the north-east, it is probable, that it may advance even beyond the banks of Newfoundland, before it is reduced to the colder temperature of the fluid beneath it, which must be flowing from the northern regions of condensation towards the points of greatest rarefaction and evaporation between the tropics, to supply the place of that, which the heat is as constantly evaporating and rarefying ; and so sending back in the upper strata of the atmosphere, to the colder regions.— The gulf-stream, thus propelled by lateral pressure, up towards the banks of Newfoundland, is seldom found to affect a ship, beyond those banks ; at the same time, it is possible, that some of it may advance farther to the northward, before that reduction is effected in its temperature, which gives it a tendency to the southward.

For, many articles, the produce of tropical climes, and
some, *known* to have been from the West Indies, have
been cast ashore on the coasts of Europe. Some of
these places being situated to the N.E. of Newfoundland, it is difficult to believe that these articles could
have been driven thither by the winds, and the swell of
the sea *only*. For these, prevailing nearly as much from
N.W. as S.W., would give them about an east direction. And if they were immersed sufficiently to feel the
influence of the great *underflow* of cold fluid, from
the north, which brings the icebergs down to 39° or
40° of latitude, they would move in an east-southerly direction.   It seems therefore reasonable to suppose, that
there may still be the remains of a northerly movement
of water at, and very near the surface, to cause bodies
floating there to make a course, as some *have done*, to
the northward of even E.N.E. from Newfoundland.
The great body of the gulf-stream is, however, much
reduced in temperature about the banks of Newfoundland ; and in proportion as it feels the cold of the great
underflow from the north, it is turned gradually to the
eastward and southward, past the Western Islands.
Whether any part of it reaches the coast of England,
France, Portugal, or Spain, is a point much disputed.
It is possible, however, that it may ; diverging, as it
appears to do, to the eastward, and southward.   Some
of the fluid that composed it *may* find its way to the
northward of Cape Finisterre, and add something to the
great body of water which the western swell heaves
into the Bay of Biscay ; and proceeding to the northward, along the coast of France, sets over from Ushant
beyond Cape Clear ; till meeting with a fluid below, of
a colder degree than its own, it perhaps gradually joins
the Polar stream to the southward, according to its depth

and temperature. Some of the waters of the gulf stream, it is possible (though hardly that), may assist in supply‑ ing the water expended by evaporation in the Mediter‑ ranean, whose surface, *therefore*, it is presumed, must be lower than that of the Atlantic, as the constant current setting into it seems to prove. Some philosophers, indeed, suppose that the quantity of water, continually admitted through the gut of Gibraltar into the Mediter‑ ranean, is greater than can be expended by evapora‑ tion ; and that, therefore, there must be a counter current setting out *underneath.* To establish this opinion, it seems necessary, first, to prove that the temperature of the Mediterranean is lower generally than that of the Atlantic. For if it be higher (as is most probable), the *surplus*, if there were any, and allowing their surfaces to be equal" (and Phoca should have added, their *specific‑ gravities the same*), " would, I presume, run out at the sur‑ face, and the supply be received in underneath, which is contrary to fact. Though I have supposed it barely possible that some of the gulf stream may cross the At‑ lantic, I by no means say that it is so. On the contrary, it is little felt by ships, far to the eastward of the Azores ; but in the vicinity of those islands, the south‑ east portion of it gradually turns to the southward, and as it advances in that direction, soon feeling the impulse again of the grand equinoctial current, is com‑ pelled to partake of its western motion : thus forming a sort of circular eddy, which may be comprised between the latitude of about 18° or 19° North, and the parallel of the Western Islands ; and from about the longitude of 29° to 43° West. Within these limits, the gulf weed is found, floating on the surface, where I suppose it origi‑ nates, lives its appointed time, and decays, like any other vegetable production ; and I believe it is rarely

Data.   C or never met with beyond these limits. Though I have admitted the bare possibility, that some of the gulf stream may enter the strait of Gibraltar, I cannot agree with the writer of the article in the Quarterly Review, when he says (speaking of the gulf stream), that it is of sufficient force and quantity to make its influence be felt in the distant 'Strait of Gibraltar.' Thus, implying (if I understand him right), that this 'force and quantity' of the gulf stream are primary causes of the constant current into the strait. On the contrary, thinking, as I do, that the causes of this constant flow of water into the Mediterranean are of a purely local nature, connect-ed exclusively with that sea ; I therefore think it most probable that if the great equinoctial current flowed (as I presume it would, were there a sufficient passage) through the Continent of America, into the Pacific ; and conse-quently annihilated the present gulf stream, there would still be the *very* same flow of water into the Mediter-ranean as there is now, as long as the sun's power con-tinued, and the localities exclusively belonging to that sea remained the same. In short, I am of opinion that the waters of the Atlantic (approximate to the Strait of Gibraltar) feel the influence of purely Mediterranean causes ; and that neither ' the force' nor ' quantity' of the gulf stream have any effect whatever in causing the current that runs into the Mediterranean. It is well known, by experience, that this current is strongest with easterly gales ; in the hottest weather, *with wind* at the same time ; and is diminished during the prevalence of westerly winds, and is weaker in winter generally than in summer.' But to return :—The winds and sur-

' The opinions of men of science are still divided as to the cause of the constant current which runs into the Mediterranean, through the strait of Gibraltar. In turning over the Annual Register for the year 1760,

face currents in the Pacific Ocean are influenced, generally, in a similar way, by the sun's power, as those

a short time ago, I observed an essay, written by Mr. Waiz, of the Royal Society of Stockholm, to explain this cause. It is ingenious, but not quite satisfactory, because his facts are at variance with each other. Mr. Waiz computes that " the water, which is received annually into the Mediterranean, by the straits, and from the Nile, and all the rivers which fall into the Black Sea, and flow through the strait of Constantinople, cannot raise its surface less than *thirty feet :* and the annual evaporation to lower it about *forty-four* feet." He then says that " *if* the Mediterranean had lost annually, since it first existed, this quantity of water, by evaporation, it would, long before now, have been reduced to a vast mass of indurated salt." And yet, he adds, " in the many thousand years, since this sea has been known, this metamorphosis has not taken place, but even its waters, as far as we know, are not become more salt." He therefore feels himself obliged to give up evaporation, and " seek some other expedient to get rid of its *redundant* waters." What redundant waters ? Has he not computed the evaporation to be sufficient to lower its surface 44 feet, and its supply through the strait of Gibraltar, and the Dardanelles, as well as by all the rivers, which flow into it, as only sufficient to raise it annually 30 feet ? Thus, so far from there being any redundancy of water in the Mediterranean, an annually increased supply would be required, and not an expedient to get rid of what he himself proves it cannot have. The expedient he has recourse to, however, is a double current, which he first proposes to *ascertain* with all possible exactness, and then to reconcile it to the laws of hydrostatics. As a proof (to him) of the existence of this *under* current, from east to west, out of the Mediterranean (which he assumes to be salter and heavier), he mentions (and others have repeated it) a story of a " Dutch transport vessel having been beaten to pieces by a French ship of war, in the middle of the strait of Gibraltar, between Tariffa and Tangier ; the wreck of this vessel, with some casks, and other *light* things, appeared, after some days, on the surface of the water, four English miles to the *west*, towards the Spanish sea." Mr. Waiz then observes, " If the direction of the current were the same at the *bottom*, as on the surface, from west to east, these wrecks could not have *raised themselves*, against the current, so as to swim at top." If we may here assume that Mr. Waiz believed, that this wreck, with the casks and other

between Africa and America, making however due
allowance for the difference of the formation and posi-

light things, did not float on the surface, but immediately *sunk* down
to the *Bottom* (the term he uses), or at least into a fluid of that degree of saltness and gravity which (as he afterwards attempts to prove,
by experiment) must give it a direction to the west, and carry these
light articles along with it,—I would ask, then, If the fluid at the surface were, as *he* must allow, less salt, or specifically lighter than that
beneath it, in proportion to its depth, yet still how *could* these *light*
articles sink to that convenient depth, unless *their* specific gravity was
greater than it?" And if greater (which however can hardly be admitted), by what law could they, when carried far enough to the westward, *as conveniently raise themselves* again to the surface, and be
observed floating in a medium, that could not support them before?

But the truth is, the fact, if it be one, proves, if it prove any
thing (taking it for granted, that the *light* substances specified would
have floated in the surface fluid), that they must have been driven
within the influence of that *surface* counter current, which every man
who has had experience in the strait of Gibraltar, knows, does set to
the *westward*, close in, both on the Barbary and Spanish shores.

Mr. Waiz, on the authority of Count Marsigli, assumes the existence of an under and surface current (in opposition to each other)
through the strait of Constantinople. He says, "that the salt water
enters at the bottom into the Black Sea, and is then rendered lighter
by the quantity of fresh water that runs into it ; after which, it flows
again in the same strait, above the salt water, into the Mediterranean,
as is seen in the strait of Gibraltar." He also says, "The currents
are stronger at Constantinople than at Gibraltar, because the difference in the degrees of saltness, of the water which comes in and that
which goes out, is greater, namely, according to Marsigli, 73 to 62 ;
whereas it is not so great in the strait of Spain."

The theory of this under current, in the strait of Gibraltar, is
thus explained by Mr. Waiz: "As there is a continual and copious
discharge of salt water into the Mediterranean, a great part of this
water deposits its salt by evaporation ; therefore what is left always
remains more salt, and consequently more weighty. *Supposing* then
the surfaces of the two seas, the Atlantic and the Mediterranean, to
be *equal*" (a supposition, however, without facts to support it), "their
gravity would not be equal ; but the water of the Mediterranean, as the

tions of intervening lands. For these obstruct the uniform general tendency of the winds and currents

most weighty, would press on that of the Atlantic, and the two seas would run together, till the waters became of equal weight, so that the Mediterranean would necessarily be lowest. When this happens, the water of the Atlantic, which is highest, cannot take its course through the strait but by a higher current, by means of which it spreads itself in the Mediterranean; but this would augment the weight, already the greatest, of the water of the latter, which cannot get away, but by opening itself a passage underneath, and forming an inferior opposite current in the strait. This is *sufficient* to produce the two currents, and to perpetuate them without interruption."

The experiment to prove this hypothesis to be in agreement with the laws of hydrostatics, is then thus described by Mr. Waiz. "Take a long box, divided into two by a board fixed in the middle; let there be a small hole in the board which you can shut at pleasure. Fill one end of the box with water, and the other with oil, to an *equal height*. On hastily opening the hole, in the board that divides them, the water, which is the heaviest, will be seen to run into the end of the box where the oil is. On the contrary, the oil will be carried in the same manner, and at the same time, into that end where the water is, over which it will spread itself. It may indeed be objected, that, as oil cannot mix with water, it must get at top, but the same thing happens to two waters of unequal gravity, when one is coloured and much salter than the other."

This hypothesis of Mr. Waiz stands on pretty sure ground, and may be applicable to the Mediterranean, *if* its waters are proved to be *salter*, and consequently heavier, than those of the Atlantic. Some philosophers, taking *this* for granted, have adopted and supported it, in preference to that of Dr. Halley, who was of opinion that the quantity of water evaporated from the Mediterranean, exceeds the supply every way necessary to equalize its surface with that of the Atlantic. *This* Mr. Waiz also admits to be the fact; and sets out by *proving* it.

Colonel Capper, whose "Observations on the Winds and Monsoons," though published in the year 1801 I never happened to meet with till last week, says, at page 202, on this question of evaporation being the cause: "In summer the land is always much hotter than water, and the surrounding air on land is much more dry; consequently the

from east to west; therefore from the east coast of
New Holland to the east coast of Africa, and within

evaporation of all Mediterranean or inland seas must be infinitely
geater than that of the ocean, in the same parallels, where the air is
already saturated, and continues in the same temperature many days
successively. Besides, it must be remembered, that the water evaporated from Mediterranean seas, is immediately in summer conveyed towards the land, where great part of it remains, being there precipitated in rain, for the benefit of the earth, or retained on the summit of
the mountains in the form of ice and snow ; and even the remainder
is but slowly returned into the different seas and lakes, through the
channels of the adjacent rivers. The quantity of water thus raised in
vapour, and retained there, for these beneficial purposes, can only be
supplied by a constant current from that part of the north Atlantic,
with which it immediately communicates.

"Should this hypothesis, on further examination, be considered as
well founded, it will serve also to account for the equatorial currents ;
for during the equinoxes, and for some weeks preceding and following
them, the evaporation near the equator must be very considerable ;
the water adjacent will therefore flow in to supply the deficiency, and
consequently in *all parts* of the ocean, where it is not obstructed by
land, will produce, at this season, opposite currents from *the two poles
to the equator*. But an exact account of the currents in the Atlantic,
kept for one year, would verify or refute this system ; and the strength
of the current at different seasons, from the ocean to the Mediterranean, through the strait of Gibraltar, would afford very useful information on this subject."

Among those who appear to have adopted the theory of Mr. Waiz,
is a writer in a popular critical review, No. 28, for May 1816. He says :
"We mean not to support the truth of Dr. Halley's theory ; we know it
is liable to a multitude of objections, from which the old *notion* of an
under current, setting out of the strait, is entirely free ; and *if* it has
been proved experimentally, what should be the case theoretically,
that the water of the Mediterranean is more salt, and consequently of
greater specific gravity than that of the Atlantic, it is as necessary
that the former should rush out underneath, and the latter rush in
above, as that the flame of a candle should be driven by the cold air
through [*under*] the bottom of a door into the room, while the more
rarefied air carries it outward at the top of the door. This under

the limits of the sun's declination, the winds and currents are periodical, according to his place. But it

current, *and* the two lateral currents which Tofino" (and every one has) " found constantly setting outwards, along the shores of Europe and Africa, at new and full moon, afford a more satisfactory solution of the problem, than the unequal effect of evaporation."

Now it appears to me that all the *facts* we do know are in favour of Dr. Halley's theory, and against that of a counter under current, which is tenable only after it shall be proved that the surfaces of the Mediterranean and Atlantic ever were, or are, equal; and that the waters of the former are specifically heavier (and colder too) at equal depths than those of the Atlantic.

At present, these two necessary data are little better than suppositions. But sound arguments are not to be built on suppositions. The first supposition, Mr. Waiz, in particular, had no claim to make as a groundwork for his hypothesis : for he sets out with computing " the quantity of evaporation as sufficient to *lower* the surface of the Mediterranean about 44 *feet* annually ; but the supply received into it, as only sufficient to *raise* it 30 *feet* annually." So that by his own showing, so far from his being entitled to suppose the surfaces of the Mediterranean and Atlantic to be, or ever to have been, equal; that of the former, if his computation were correct, would have been lowered 14 feet, every succeeding year. Now, so great a disparity between the annual supply of water to the Mediterranean, and its expenditure by *some cause*, be it what it may, is disproved by past and present experience. For no such diminution of the water in the Mediterranean has taken place. Its surface is of the same height nearly as it has been in all ages. That its surface *is lower* generally than that of the Black Sea, and of the Atlantic, we want no calculation to show : the constant flow of the first through the Strait of Constantinople, and of the Atlantic *into it* through the Gut of Gibraltar, are facts before our eyes which prove it agreeably to the laws of hydrostatics. And according to the same laws, *if* ever the supply to the Mediterranean should so far exceed the expenditure by evaporation, as to *realize* Mr. Waiz's supposititious theory of equal surfaces, then the effect he showed by his box experiment may take place, *provided* the waters of the Mediterranean *be* specifically heavier, salter, and colder, at equal depths, than those of the Atlantic. But if they are nearly of equal specific gravity (which, notwithstanding a few partial experiments to the contrary,

would be leading us too far out of the way, to attempt
to trace the currents in the Indian seas, influenced as
they are, so variously, and oppositely, in their direction
and velocity, at different seasons, by the Monsoons and
the bodies of land within their limits. Suffice it to say
what more particularly applies to the North Pacific, and
will lead us again to the Arctic regions.

" Having said, that the air is rarefied and raised in
the atmosphere, and that the greatest degree of evaporation is effected between the west coast of Africa, and
the east coast of America; and that *north* of the line, the
fluid is so returned *towards* the North Pole, and being
condensed somewhere in its passage by cold, it perhaps
supplies with water some of the rivers which discharge
into the seas of the temperate zone or into the North
Polar Ocean ; and, whether falling in rain, hail, or snow,
upon the earth or not, it ultimately finds its way into
the Ocean. And according to the temperature propor-
tionate to its depth, the water takes a direction towards
the regions of equatorial heat ; is again raised by that
heat to the surface, and again evaporated. Experiments
in the *Ocean* have proved, that when the temperature
of the atmosphere *exceeds* that of the surface of the sea,
the superficial water is generally warmer than that at
certain depths *beneath* it (I say *generally*, because *in
soundings*, and confined waters, local causes effect many

is probably the case), and the surface of the Mediterranean be at all
times *lower* than that of the Atlantic, then the perpetual flow of the
surface of the latter into the Mediterranean must be the consequence,
as certainly as any other effect follows its proper antecedent cause.
Nay, even if the Red Sea had any channel of communication with the
Mediterranean, *its* waters also would flow into it, because the surface
of the Red Sea, I should suppose, *must* be higher than that of the other,
for obvious reasons."

exceptions to this general rule), and, in all probability, the greater the depth the *colder* the fluid in *that case*. And as we know that when the air (or water) receives an increase of heat, its parts will be put in motion towards that heat, it follows, that the colder water throughout its whole depth must have a tendency to flow towards the point of greatest heat, and therefore be continually rising towards the surface in the equatorial regions.— This probably is the routine of the general movement of the atmosphere, and the waters of the Ocean, between Europe, Africa, and America, and from the arctic regions to the equator.[1]   And it seems no less probable;

[1] Colonel Capper, in his " Observations on the Winds and Monsoons," says, at page 130, " In the next place, I shall attempt to show by what means the atmosphere is supplied with water; in what manner the winds are rendered the vehicle for conveying this moisture to the earth ; and by what means these waters are again returned to the sea, carrying with them the salts from the land, so as to keep up the saltness of the ocean.

" In the absence of the sun in the winter solstice, immense masses of ice and snow are collected, in the polar regions, which by these means become so many reservoirs of water, deposited there by the hand of Nature, in a solid form, until the return of the sun, when they are in part dissolved, and being again put in circulation, serve to increase the quantity of the water in the sea.

" During the whole of the summer solstice, in each hemisphere, including the three hottest months, the quantity of ice and snow thus dissolved must be prodigious.   If when this operation is performing the sun was suddenly to disappear, and this mass of water to be again immediately congealed, the first dissolution would have taken place in vain : but the course of the sun is gradual, and as he continues his progress, either north or south, one atmosphere is progressively warmed, whilst the other is proportionably cooled : with the former a vacuum is formed, which is filled up by the cold denser air put in motion by its gravity to restore the equilibrium : this motion of the air consequently conveys with it the increased body of water *from* the *polar regions,* and carries this additional mass *towards the tropics and the equator.*

Data.   D

that in the Pacific they are subject to the same general laws. For there also the great equatorial current is in constant motion to the westward; and like the gulfstream, and from causes, too, in *some* points similar, it gradually turns to the northward when it approaches the lands to the northward of New Guinea and the Philippine Islands, being perhaps at the same time influenced by currents setting in a different direction; more particularly during the prevalence of the southwest monsoon in the Indian and China seas. Near the coast of Japan the current has been found to set N.E. by N., at the rate of five miles an hour: at 18 leagues distance, about three knots, in the same direction; but at a greater distance from the land it inclined more to the eastward; and at 60 leagues from the land it set E.N.E., three miles an hour; then (like the gulf-stream) inclining gradually to the southward; so that at the distance of 120 leagues from the coast of Nipon, its direction was S.E., and its rate not more than a knot. From this current setting generally to the N.E., along the coast of Japan, more or less strong, according to the season of the year, it appears that the motion of the air and waters, between the west coast of America and New Holland, and all the lands northward towards Behring's Strait, is *similar* to that north of the Equator, between Africa, Europe and America. It is therefore presumable, that though a *superficial* current may run into Behring's Strait, there must also be one running *out* of it *underneath,* if there be no obstruc-

"When the *polar* currents of air *and water,* if we may use this expression, reach the torrid zone, the constant heat of the sun, which is increased likewise by the heat of the earth as it approaches the land, causes a considerable increase of evaporation, or in common language, a distillation of the sea water, leaving behind in the ocean all its saline qualities."

tion, and the principles this theory rests on are *correct*.
But the writer of the article I am examining is of opinion that 'the constant circular motion, and interchange of waters between the Pacific and the Atlantic'
must be by Behring's Strait; otherwise 'it would be difficult to explain the perpetual egress of a current from
the Polar basin into the Atlantic, without admitting a
supply through the only remaining opening into that
basin, to answer the demand of the current.' I admit
the probability of a surface current into the Strait, for
the reasons already given, and believe there may be
one, because it is mentioned thus in Cook's Voyage:
'We were now convinced that we had been under the
influence of a strong current setting to the north, that
had caused an error in our latitude of 20 miles. In
passing this Strait last year we experienced the same
effect. On the 12th of July, when within the Strait, in
latitude 69°. 37', and half way between the two continents, the current was found to set N.W. at the rate of
one knot.' This proves there was a surface current,
though a small one, both at the entrance and to the
northward of the Strait. But what have we to found
the supposition on, that the waters may be 'rushing
out' (that is, in from the Pacific, I suppose is meant)
'with the greatest violence under the *Floodgate*,' which
means 'the impenetrable barrier of ice which stopped
the progress of Cook's successors?'

"The author of the article in question supposes
that 'if the Polar basin should prove to be free from
land about the Pole, it will also be free of ice,' and
that this may be the case is not improbable, in the
summer season: not, however, because of the non-existence of land, but for other reasons, which shall be
explained by and by. He also supposes that the

barrier of ice which stopped the progress of Cook's successors was moveable, or no where touched the bottom. The writer of Cook's Voyage was of the same opinion as to the ice *nearest* the ship, though that opinion rested on a foundation that might not, perhaps, equally apply to the larger masses of ice further to the northward, and *not seen.* His words are :—' We had twice traversed the sea, in lines nearly parallel to the run we had just made, and in the first of those traverses we were not able to penetrate so far north, by eight or ten leagues, as in the second ; and that in the last, we had again found an united body of ice, generally about five leagues *to the southward* of its position in the preceding run. As this proves that the large compact fields of ice which *we saw* were moveable, or diminishing, at the same time, it does not leave any well-founded expectation of advancing much further in the most favorable season.'

"Though this proves that the floating ice *seen* shifted its position, both to the northward and to the *southward*, but *chiefly* the latter, as will be soon further proved—yet it does not prove that the larger masses to the northward, perhaps, which they did not see, might not be immoveable, by grounding on the bottom, *if* the water became *shoaler* in that direction, as our navigators found it *was*, as far as they advanced. Now should there have been any immoveable masses of ice to the northward, it would in some degree explain *why* the current, which the writer in the review supposes to set with such ' violence' from the Pacific, should not have carried the *ice* away with it towards the Pole, where there may be *none.* But, if the whole of this ice was moveable, it proves that whether there was a small current setting to the northward, or not, and whether at the surface or the bottom, or both, there must have been a *stronger* current from the northward, or *something* else, which still more powerfully impelled the ice to the southward, in defiance of the other, as well as of the wind, which appears to have been generally from the south-west when strongest. It is said in Cook's Voyage, ' It may be observed, that in the year 1778, we did not meet with the ice till we advanced to the latitude of 70°, on the 17th of August; and that then we found it in compact bodies, extending as far as the eye could reach, and of which a *part* or the whole was moveable ; since by *drifting down upon us* (from the northward) we narrowly escaped being hemmed in between it and the land.' On the Asiatic side they encountered extensive fields of ice, and were sure to meet with it about the latitude of 70°, quite across, whenever they attempted to stand to the northward. On the 26th of August they were obstructed by it in 69¼°, in such quantities as made it quite impossible to pass either to the north or west. In the second attempt they could do little more, for they were never able to approach the continent of Asia higher than 67°; nor that of America, in any part, than 68°, or 68°. 20′ north. But in the last attempt they were obstructed by the ice *three degrees further to the southward*, and their endeavors to push further to the northward were principally confined to the mid space between the two coasts.

" Now all this does not seem to *favor* the supposition of a current ' rushing in' from the Pacific through Behring's Strait, with such velocity, as it may fairly be supposed a body of water would have, of sufficient quantity to supply the southerly current, ' setting perpetually into the Atlantic on *both* sides of Greenland, not only when the ice is melting, but when the *sea is freez-ing.*' Indeed, if we do but consider for a moment the quantity of water that may be supposed to flow through so extensive a space as Davis's Strait, 'with a ve-locity of four, and sometimes even five miles an hour;' and then add to that the amazing quantity setting as constantly to the southward, in the still greater space to the eastward of Greenland and Spitzbergen, it does certainly appear to be improbable, nay, *impossible*, that a current of at least equal, or of double velocity, and occupying the full extent in depth and breadth of Behring's Strait, would be at all adequate to answer the demand; much less, so trifling a current as we are warranted by *facts* to believe there *is*. For in Cook's Voyage, the remarks on this matter are thus summed up :—' By comparing the reckoning with the observa-tions, we found the currents to set different ways, yet more from south-west than any other quarter. We again tried the currents, and found them unequal, but *never exceeding* one mile an hour. Whatever their direction might be, their effect was *so trifling*, that no conclusion respecting the existence of a passage to the northward could be drawn from them.'

It is presumed, that all the currents here spoken of were superficial; but even admitting they extended quite across the Strait, and flowed the same way throughout its whole depth, still it seems quite beyond the bounds of possibility that the quantity of water so admitted, and with a rate of flow '*so trifling*,' could be sufficient for the supply of the currents ' setting to the southward perpetually, through the other *two* open-ings, (Baffin's sea being *doubted* then) into the At-lantic.'

" Judging from such facts as are before us, that a

part, and but a very small part, of the demand to supply the southern current, comes in from the Pacific
through Behring's Strait, it is necessary to inquire, From
what sources then is all the water so flowing out of the
polar regions derived ? I have supposed the currents
to be produced (at least the motion of the great deep)
generally by evaporation in the equatorial regions of
heat, and by cold returned in various ways in the
atmosphere, by land and by sea, into the northern regions, even as far as the Pole. For though 'the way
of the Almighty is,' as the Psalmist says, ' in the sea,
and his path in the deep waters,' yet it is also as
surely in the clouds of heaven. And though his foot-
steps are not known certainly, yet it is permitted us
humbly to endeavor to trace them.

" Whether or not there be any increase of water from
the melting of the ice in the Polar sea, so as to cause a
current to the south, appears not to be very material,
and perhaps has little to do with the general quantity
in the 'Polar basin.' In all probability, it remains
nearly the same at all times, whether there is more or
less ice ; that is, taking the ice and water together to
make up that quantity. I agree with the reviewer, that
' those who could suppose the melting of the ice to
afford such a supply, would betray a degree of igno-
rance greater, perhaps, than that of not being aware
of the very little influence which an arctic summer
exerts on fields of ice, perpetually surrounded as they
are by a freezing atmosphere created by themselves !'
However, there is no subject, perhaps, on which opinions have been more at variance than on the melting
of the ice in the polar regions, as well as where and
how it is formed. St. Pierre went so far as to suppose
it was the cause of the tides ; but he does not appear

to have been a 'plain matter-of-fact man,' but of fancy and imagination.

"Others think the ice does not melt at all, or at least very little, even in summer. If ice, when once formed (be it how it may) round and along the coasts of these regions, *does not* melt at all, there must be a constant increase, so long as that ice is 'surrounded perpetually by a freezing atmosphere created by itself,' which the reviewer tells us it ' mostly is, even in summer :' and if so, we may fairly presume it *always* is in *winter*.

" At this rate, with the exception of what may make its escape through Davis's Strait, and to the eastward of Greenland, it would necessarily be always advancing towards the Pole, (admitting the land to be the place of its first formation) and close over it; unless we can find some probable cause counteracting this effect of *perpetual frost*. And perhaps we are warranted in supposing that there exists some such cause. Indeed it seems more than probable, that the process of *freezing* and *melting* may be going on in the arctic regions, on the *same* body of ice, (if of magnitude to be sufficiently immersed,) at the *same time*, and *perhaps* in the winter, as well as the summer.

" Water is a compound of ice and caloric. The temperature of ice is 32° ; and whilst surrounded by a temperature *equal*, it will remain ice. But whenever the temperature of the atmosphere exceeds 32°, and continues so long enough for the body of ice to receive a *sufficiency* of caloric to effect its dissolution, it will do so. It is probable, that the temperature of the atmosphere, even in the arctic regions, in summer *will* sometimes exceed 32°, and the more, perhaps, the nearer the Pole ; and whenever it does, *sufficiently*, the effect on ice is obvious.

" This seems sufficient to be said, on the *probability*
of ice *above* water melting in the Arctic regions in
summer, if the temperature of the atmosphere ever
sufficiently exceeds 32°. In the winter, as the temperature of the atmosphere *must* be constantly below
that, of course the freezing above water will be as
constant, though the surface of the sea itself will probably not freeze till at a temperature much below 30°,
even in a motionless state. The *same* body of ice,
whilst freezing above water, that is, increasing in size
and extent by snow, hail, and the salt water freezing
in washing over it, may perhaps, at the *same time*, be
melting under water; and this process will probably
be accelerated according to the magnitude of the mass,
and the depth of its immersion. For, when the atmosphere is colder than the surface of the sea, the
water will (in proportion, perhaps, to its depth) be
found *warmer* by some degrees, than at the surface ;
and though few experiments have yet been made to
establish the fact, yet sufficient to warrant this conclusion. Thus in summer, if the temperature of the atmosphere should be 32°, and the surface of the sea
(*clear of land and soundings*) three or four degrees
higher, that of the water *below* would probably be
much higher still; so that the portion of a large mass
of ice, *above the surface* of the sea, would remain ice,
and augment; and the other portion of it *below*, being
immersed in a temperature exceeding the point of
congelation, would probably be melting and decreasing. The well attested facts, of large bodies of ice
having been seen to capsize or turn bottom up, prove
that their centres of gravity are altered, by either an
increase of their bulk above, or a diminution of it
below, according to the excess of either effect. Upon

Data.   E

the whole, however, it seems probable, that in the Arctic regions the process of freezing in the atmosphere exceeds that of melting under water, particularly on those smaller masses of ice which are immersed the least, and therefore there must be a *general increase* of ice in the ' Polar basin,' from the Pole (if the ice originates there) towards the lands surrounding the ' basin ;' or from those lands (if the ice first forms there) up towards the Pole. On this question, too, opinions have been various. Every circumstance seems to weigh against the opinion of its greatest formation being about the Pole, except one, and that is, because the sea water there will probably contain least salt. I am disposed to believe that it must also be much colder in the *winter*, at the surface of the sea *near the Pole*, than any where else. In the part of the Polar basin further to the southward, where it is bounded by land, it is to be presumed that the general prevailing winds are from S.W. to N.W., particularly the former, in bad weather ; northerly, and easterly, when most settled and fine. *If so*, it is to be supposed there will be a current generally prevailing from the westward to the eastward, partaking at the same time of that general tendency of the fluid to move *southward* from the Pole, which I imagine it will be found to have, from the *coldness* of *its* temperature " [meaning, I suppose, as compared with the progressively increasing general temperature of the sea from the Pole towards the Equator]. "These two general combined impulses, operating on moveable bodies, floating on the surface of the Arctic seas, must impel them in an *east-southerly* direction, all round the globe : being, in fact, that ' circumvolving current,' which the reviewer mentions, ' as carrying fir, larch, aspen, and other trees, the produce of both Asia and America, from the Polar basin through the outlet into the northern ocean." The ' puzzling' diagram, as Phoca terms it, as well as the remarks he makes on the reviewer's ingenuity, in having so happily ' assisted ' the reader in the explanation of the notions *he* entertained on this interesting subject, I do not deem it necessary to repeat here. Phoca continues : " Having, for the reasons before given, presumed, that there is a circumvolving current in the Arctic sea, from west to east, but *southerly withal,* it leads me to inquire into the probable effect of *it,* and the winds together, upon floating masses of ice.

" In the first place, (let the ice be formed where it may) its *general* direction will in all probability be from west to east, with a tendency at the same time to set to the *southward,* too strong to be counteracted by the force of any winds from *that* quarter ; its bulk under being greater than that above the surface.

" If we cast our eyes on a chart of the north Polar regions, no opening is seen for the egress of ice to the *southward,* out of the ' Polar basin,' from Norway and Lapland to the eastward, along the whole coast of Asia, till we come to Behring's Strait. Through *this* strait it does not appear at all probable that much of the ice *can* pass, on account of its comparative small extent ; and the depth of water being perhaps insufficient to float the bodies of greatest magnitude. There may also be ' a trifling current,' as I suppose ; or one of the ' greatest violence,' as the Quarterly Reviewer supposes, running in from the Pacific, to oppose its passage through the Strait.

" From Behring's Strait, then, all along the coast of America, we find no opening for the ice to escape till we get to ' Baffin's Sea !' and Davis's Strait. Through this Strait, *if there be* an uninterrupted communication, it is not unfair to presume that immense quantities *would* be carried by a current 'running perpetually with a velocity, *as* it is *stated*, of four, and sometimes of even five miles an hour !' I am, however, inclined to think, that either from the interruption of *lands*, or shoals, between Greenland and America, a comparative small quantity passes from the 'Polar basin' through Davis's Strait ; and that much of the ice, as well as currents, *may* have Hudson's Bay for their origin. *If* any obstruction *do* exist to the free egress of ice through Davis's Strait, the consequence must be a vast accumulation of it, in a mass more or less consolidated, from about Nova Zembla, all the way to the eastward, *as far* as *Greenland*, and extending northward from every part of the coasts of Asia and America, at least *to the parallel* of latitude in which the *north point of Greenland may lie.* For whatever masses of ice cannot pass through Davis's Strait must be pressed continually by others, brought from the westward and northward, by the circumvolving current, along the north part of the more connected ice.

" If its progress to the southward, through Davis's Strait, were not SOMEHOW *impeded, it would* pass through. If impeded in its course to the southward (let the impediment be what it may), it is yet still more impeded in its progress to the eastward, by the west side of Greenland ; and therefore *must* accumulate against this solid barrier, *as far* at least to the *northward* as Greenland extends. Then, and not till then, can ice of any comparative quantity drive further to the eastward, or find *any* passage down to the southward. All the ice farthest to the northward of Greenland is then at liberty to move on towards Spitzbergen ; whilst the ice that may be in motion closest in with the land, when rounding the north-east part of Greenland, will take a turn to the southward, and *in towards* the coast withal ; because it will be within the influence of an eddy, that must necessarily be produced in the stream of waters passing *nearest* to the north-east part of that land. *There* it must collect, and if it consolidate, extend to the shores of Iceland, or even Spitzbergen ; or else ' burst its fetters,' as it is said to have done lately, and drift away to the southward, into the Atlantic.

"This is sufficient to account for the ice between Greenland and Spitzbergen having a general movement to the south-west. And there is the same reason to suppose, that the ice nearest to the north-east and east coast of Spitzbergen, has also a similar movement. But it will not warrant the conclusion, of there being a current in the same direction, at any considerable distance to the northward and eastward of Spitzbergen. On the contrary, it seems most probable, that any masses of ice found in that direction, to the northward of 82° or 83°, will be more within the influence of the *general* circumvolving current ; and therefore make an east-southerly drift towards Nova Zembla, and perhaps clear of its NE. point. Greenland and Spitzbergen, being situated so much further to the northward than any other known land in the Arctic regions, form an impenetrable barrier against the movement, to the eastward, of any ice but what may be to the *northward* of them both.

" Much of this northernmost *surplus* ice finding its way to the southward, is one reason why it seems very likely, that ice in the greatest quantity, and most compact, will be found from about Nova Zembla, all along

the coasts of Asia and America, and extending to the
northward as far, generally, as the *north* part of
Greenland ; and that, perhaps, less and less ice will
be found to the northward of its parallel, as the Pole is
approached. That is, adopting the opinion that the
ice is first produced near the surrounding lands, and
accumulated afterwards at sea, so as to extend its surface from those lands northerly till it reaches the parallel of the *north* point of Greenland, which the surplus
ice *must round*, before it *can* pass into the Atlantic, *if*
Davis's Strait *be obstructed*.

" Greenland and Spitzbergen forming so powerful a
bar to the progress of the ice to the eastward, with the
circumvolving current, renders it extremely probable
that there is always less ice between Nova Zembla and
Spitzbergen than any where else in the same parallel,
and *perhaps* still less, the nearer the Pole in *summer*.

" Whether the ice during the winter encompasses the
Pole or not, can only be matter of conjecture ; and, in
all probability, the fact will never be decided by man.
In that season, if the cold is intense in proportion to
the nearness to the Pole, it is possible the ice may advance to it. But yet, as it is more probably drifted
out of the ' Polar basin,' as fast as it collects, to the
northward of Greenland, it seems more reasonable to
conclude that it seldom reaches beyond the latitude of
82° or 83°, in any very extensive or consolidated bodies,
all the year round. On this ground, for one, rests the
opinion I hold in common with the writer of the article
in question, of the probability of the vicinity of the Pole
being free of ice *in the summer* ; not, however, as a consequence of there being no land there, but whether
there shall be any land or not. For I have supposed
it likely, that the temperature of the atmosphere, in the

Arctic regions, *sometimes* may exceed 32°; and the more, perhaps, the nearer the Pole is approached. First, because there may be less ice, for the reasons I have given.—And if there *be* ice, there will *probably* be a warmer atmospheric temperature, to dissolve it, at the Pole itself, than any where else to the southward of it, as far as 80° or 75°: because, when the sun's rays first strike the Pole, they will be felt there incessantly for six months; but with what force and effect, we have yet to learn. On all other parallels, in proportion to their distances from the Pole, the duration of the sun's influence will be shorter. And though the sun's power, during the periods they feel it, may perhaps be greater than at the Pole, yet being interrupted whilst he is below the horizon, it is perhaps probable, on *the whole*, that the greatest effect of the sun's heat may be at the Pole; as, there, he is above the horizon for six months; in the latitude of 84°, about five months; and in 78½, about four months only at a time.

"We are next to inquire, what facility the late disappearance of the ice from the east coast of Old Greenland offers—first, for attempting a direct passage over the Pole; and secondly, the more circuitous one, along the northern coast of America, into the Pacific.

"As to the first, according to the view I have taken of the subject, it appears to me that the facility this event offers for attempting a direct passage over the Pole, would be very *nearly the same*, whether more or less ice be collected, not only on the eastern coast of Old Greenland, but *all round* it, and even between it and Iceland, and towards Spitzbergen. That is, *provided the attempt is to be made*, as it is to be hoped it will be, to the *eastward of Spitzbergen;* because, for the reasons I have offered, it is *probable the least quantity of ice* will be found *there, clear of the land.* At all events, whatever masses may be found there, they will in all probability be of less magnitude, and more detached from each other, because the space for them to move in is least confined. If any of the vessels fitting out be destined to take *this route,* the probability is, that *if* they advance beyond the latitude of 82° or 83° north, the ice will less and less impede their progress to the Pole ; and to reach it will perhaps be the least difficult part of the enterprise. To the northward of 82° or 83°, up to the Pole, it is likely that the weather in the summer will be for the most part fine, but hazy generally. Thick fogs will be frequent. The winds are likely to be moderate, shifting often round from north to east, by south, to west, and north again, but prevailing chiefly from the eastward and northward. *If* our Polar navigator pass the Pole without any great difficulty, and find the true south course he has steered to be on or near the 170° west meridian, and so leading him towards Behring's Strait, he will, in all probability, soon get to the southward as far as 80°, or perhaps 78°, where it is as probable he will find his *further progress stopped* by ice, perhaps impenetrable.

" From *this part* of the expedition, therefore, *I* see no very reasonable ground for entertaining ' lively hopes,' that a practicable passage for *ships* will be discovered into the Pacific, though there does not seem to be the least doubt of there being one for *water and fish.*

" As to the second, viz. ' the more circuitous passage, along the north coast of America into the Pacific,' the prospect of success is still more *unfavorable* than the other ; because the navigators are destined, in the first place, ' to struggle against the ice, currents, and tides, in Davis's Strait, and on the east coast of America, which the writer of the article I have been examining tells us himself 'are of course never free from *mountains* and patches of ice;' and to which *he* attributes the failure in every attempt, either to make *this (very)* passage, or to 'ascertain its impracticability;' so that the highest point former navigators ever reached is the arctic circle, or at most the 67th parallel!' But even allowing that the present adventurers do reach the north-east point of America, and discover a passage through what is 'gratuitously called Baffin's Bay,' they will then have to make no less than one hundred degrees of westing, most probably through immense fields of ice, fixed, or moving with the circumvolving current as well as the winds, both prevailing in a general direction from west to east, *against them.* If there be any ground to hope that a practicable passage for *ships can* be discovered between the Pacific and the Atlantic, along the north coast of America, the chances are, that it will be done (if ever it be) *from* Behring's Strait to the eastward ; and therefore, it is much more likely to be accomplished by the Russian officers, said to be making the attempt this year, than by ours ; because most of the obstacles opposed to the progress of our navigators, from east to west, will be *in favor* of the Russians the other way."

It appears in the preface to Captain Ross's account of his unsuccessful Voyage, that as early as the 4th of December, 1817, he was informed that two ships were to be sent out to ascertain the existence or non-existence of a north-west passage. On the 15th of January, 1818, four ships were commissioned, viz. the Isabella, Alexander, Dorothea, and Trent; the two former for the north-west, and the latter two for the Polar expeditions. On the 16th of April the Isabella and Alexander reached the Nore, and on the 25th their pilots quitted them off Cromer. The Dorothea and Trent joined them at Lerwick on the 1st of May, but did not accompany them to sea on the 3d. The instructions to Captain Ross, who commanded the N.W. expedition, (as exhibited in his account of his Voyage) were dated on the 31st March, 1818 ; and from their general tenor it would seem that the Quarterly Reviewer had been consulted, and many of his suggestions adopted, as to the most eligible route to be pursued. The reviewer denied, or at least doubted the existence of the land seen by Baffin, and what had been hitherto ' gratuitously called Baffin's Bay;' and assumed the belief of an open sea to the northward of Davis's Strait, and the existence of a ' perpetual current through that Strait, from the northward, with a velocity of four, and sometimes even of five miles an hour.' In conformity with these assumptions, Captain Ross is instructed, in the first place, ' to make the best of his way into Davis's Strait, through which he will endeavor to pass to *the northward*, without stopping on either of its coasts, unless he should find it absolutely necessary.' The instructions add—' From the best information we have been able to obtain, it would appear that a current of some force runs from the northward towards the upper part of Davis's Strait, during the summer season, and perhaps for most part of the winter also. This current, if it be considerable, can scarcely be altogether supplied by streams from the land, or the melting of ice ; there would therefore seem reason to suppose it may be derived from an *open sea*, in which case Baffin's Bay cannot be bounded by land.' The reviewer supposes, as we have seen in a former page, that the north-east point of America may be situated in latitude from 70°

to 72° N., and says, that all former attempts at a north
west passage failed, because none of them were ever
made near that part of the coast; but he apprehends
difficulty in approaching it by way of *narrow Straits*, as
' they are generally choked up with ice, which incon-
venience would be obviated by standing first to the
northward to the latitude of 71° or 72°.' Agreeably to
this, it is suggested ' in the instructions to Captain
Ross,' as a general observation, that a passage through
fields of ice is most likely to be found where the sea
is *deepest*, and *least connected with land ;* as there is
reason to suppose that ice is found to be *more abundant*
near the shores *of the continent and islands*, in *narrow
straits*, and deep bays.' By the by, I wonder
whether this observation (which is really a very sound
one) suggested itself to the person (whoever he was)
who drew up the instructions for Captain Buchan, to
pursue *his* course in the ' Dorothea and Trent, in a direction as due north as may be found practicable
through the Spitzbergen seas.' If it had, that officer
would in all probability have been more fortunate in
making his attempt to the *eastward* of Spitzbergen, for
the reasons given by Phoca, and which the reviewer
himself must admit to be correct, even on *his own* principle ; though to be sure the reviewer says, ' The failure of the Polar expedition was owing to *one* of those
accidents to which all sea voyages are liable, more especially when to the ordinary sea risk is superadded
that of a navigation among fields and masses of ice.'
Captain Ross is further instructed, after reaching ' that
part of the sea to the northward of Davis's Strait'
which, if reports may be relied on, is generally free
from ' field ice,' to stand well to the northward before he
edge away to the westward, in order to get a good

offing, in rounding the north-east point of the continent
of America ; whose latitude has not been ascertained,
but which, if a conjecture may be hazarded, from what
is known of the northern coast of that continent, may
perhaps be found in or about the 72nd degree of latitude.'
' In the event of his being able to succeed in rounding
this point, and finding the sea open,' he is instructed
' *carefully to avoid* coming *near the coast, where* he would
be most likely to be *impeded* by *fixed* or *floating ice ;*
but, keeping well to the northward, and in deep water,
to make the best of his way to Behring's Strait.'

After these expeditions had sailed, two more articles
appeared on the question of this north-west passage ;
one in the Quarterly Review, No. 36, for June, 1818,
in *favor* of its accomplishment of course ; and the
other in the Edinburgh, No. 69, for the same month,
quite as full of that ' scepticism,' which its more *or-
thodox* opponent approves of—not in ' matters of religion'—but of ' science, which, by provoking inquiry,
frequently leads to the detection of error, and always
stimulates to the discovery of truth.'

As some passages in *both* these rival reviews appear
to have occasioned a more than common quantum of
this *laudable* scepticism on the mind of Phoca, he was
induced to publish another letter in the Naval Chro-
nicles for September and October, before the two expeditions returned ; being 'An Attempt to prove, from
Circumstances and Facts stated by Philosophers, that
a Passage *for Ships* from the ' *Polar Basin*' to the Pacific through Behring's Strait, *must* be impracticable.'

" Mr. Editor,   Hull, 5th Sept. 1818.
" Locke tells us, that ' false or doubtful positions,
relied upon as unquestionable maxims, keep those in

the dark from truth who build on them ; and to be indifferent which of two opinions is true, is the right temper of mind that preserves it from being imposed upon, and disposes it to examine with that indifferency until it has done its best to find out the truth ; and this is the only direct and safe way to it.'

" In examining subjects of science and philosophy, as well as of religion, this indifferency is particularly requisite ; and the mind should be entirely divested of that prejudice by which individuals as well as parties are so liable to be misled.

" On a subject of the former kind, which has for the last few months attracted so much of the superficial notice and curiosity of the public, and perhaps the serious consideration of a 'few, it seems peculiarly necessary to have the mind thus prepared for its discussion—I mean the pending expeditions to explore the arctic regions. Some points connected with them, so strongly asserted, and attempted to be proved by one set of philosophers, and as strongly opposed, and denied by another, seem calculated to distract the judgment, even of those who happen to be prejudiced in 'favor of either party, without convincing any who think the matter worthy of their attention, and feel disposed, without bias, to inquire into the solidity of the arguments used by either, to prove their assertions and conjectures well founded, or stated facts to be true, which appear discordant.

" The grand and chief point, on which these philosophers are at issue, appears to be, whether Behring's Strait ' is merely the entrance of a vast bay or inland sea ?' or ' the separation of two vast continents ?' Each seeming to rest their opinion, as to the success or failure of the expeditions, mainly on that question.

" Captain Burney, in his Memoir, proposed to show, that ' there does not exist satisfactory proof of such separation ; and, secondly, from *peculiarities* which have been observed, there is cause to suppose the fact to be otherwise; that is to say, that Asia and America are contiguous, and parts of one and the same continent.'

" As it is clear that we have no positive proof of the junction of the two continents of Asia and America, let us examine the nature of those *peculiarities* from which Captain Burney concludes ' there is *cause* to suppose them contiguous, and one and the same.'

" These peculiarities were—First, 'The sudden disappearance of tides, on arriving in Behring's Strait.— Secondly, There was little or no current, nor could it be perceived that the tide either rose or fell.—Thirdly, That to the northward of the latitude of 68° 45′ N. the soundings were observed to decrease.' It will then be proper to inquire how far these ' peculiarities ' authorise the *supposition?* And lastly, whether the very same peculiarities *could* exist *if* the continents do *not join ?*

" The philosophers of the north argue in support of the supposition, chiefly on the grounds stated by Captain Burney. Those of the south not only seem to discredit the existence of the ' peculiarities ' observed personally by Captain Burney himself, but on an hypothesis of their own, as well as from some of the facts stated by that officer, they endeavor to establish their opinion of the separation of the two continents, and the existence of a perpetual current from the Pacific through Behring's Strait into the Arctic Sea ; finally declaring, that they 'have less apprehension of the passage through Behring's Strait being closed against our navigators (except by ice) than of the *difficulties* they may have to encounter on *this side of America.'*

" On the subject of currents in general, and particularly what is called the gulf-stream, as well as *this supposed* one through Behring's Strait, as asserted in the Quarterly Review before, I was induced to make a few observations on the 27th of February last. On these questions, therefore, I do not mean to enlarge here; though, regarding what has been further said, in that Review for June last, on the extraordinary effects of currents, and their *assumed* direction, I may perhaps offer a few remarks as I go along.

" The philosophers of the north have not considered it worth while to notice these points, and only observe, that 'the notion of a stream rushing beneath a frozen arch cannot be admitted.' But to return to the question of the separation or junction of Asia and America. *If* Behring's Strait *is* 'merely the entrance of a vast bay or inland sea,' the failure of both expeditions, as well by way of the Pole as Davis's Strait, must be certain, even were they to surmount all the difficulties in their progress by either route ; the object of both being to pass through that Strait into the Pacific.

" But even if Behring's Strait should be ' the separation of two great continents,' a further and no less important question arises, viz. Whether another local impediment does not exist, which must, of necessity, be *as impassable* as land, at least for *ships*, and therefore occasion some, if not all, of those very peculiarities, from the personal observation and knowledge of which, Captain Burney concludes 'there is cause to *suppose* that Asia and America are contiguous, and parts of one and the same continent.'

" Feeling no bias towards the opinions or the suppositions of either party, and regardless of the fact, either of the junction or separation of Asia and America, my object in this examination is to attempt to prove, *as far as known facts*, and other circumstances, stated and *agreed in* by both parties, *can prove*, that the passage for *ships* from the *Polar Sea* into the Pacific, by way of Behring's Strait, *is as impracticable* as if Asia and America *were known to join*. Though we are perhaps warranted in giving full credit to the account Captain Burney gives of the 'peculiarities' he observed ; yet it may be as well to examine the facts stated in Cook's and Clarke's Voyages, in support of his evidence; as well as some of the circumstances mentioned in the Quarterly Review in refutation of it.

" The first fact noticed by Captain Burney is ' the sudden disappearance of tides on arriving in Behring's Strait ;' and the second, that 'there was little or no current ; nor could it be perceived that the tide either rose or fell.'

" In Clarke's Voyage it is stated, that ' on Thursday the 1st of July, Mr. Bligh, the master of the Resolution, having moored a small keg with the deep sea lead in 75 fathoms water (off Thadeus' Noss), found that the ship made a course north by east about half a mile an hour.' This was attributed by him ' to the effect of the *southerly swell*, rather than to any current.'

" In Cook's Voyage, when at anchor in 6 fathoms, with the Peaked Mountain over Cape Prince of Wales, bearing S. 10° W., on the 11th of August, it is remarked, ' We perceived *little* or *no current*, nor did we perceive that the tide either rose or fell.' Again, on the 21st of August, in lat. 69° 30', it is said, ' During the afternoon we had but little wind, and the master was sent in a boat to observe whether there was any current, but he found none.' In Clarke's Voyage, when off Cape East, on the 5th of July, it is remarked, ' We were now convinced of our having been under the influence of a strong current, setting *to the north,* which had occasioned an error of 20 miles in the computation of the latitude at noon. At the time of our passing the Strait last year, we experienced a similar effect.' On Monday, the 12th of July, in latitude 69° 49′ N. within the Strait, on the Asiatic side, it is remarked :—' On examining the current, we found it to set north-west, at the rate of half a mile an hour.' And finally, in describing the local circumstances generally, within the Strait, the account of the tide or current is thus given:—' We found but little tide or current, and that little came from the *westward ;*' that is, *athwart* the Strait's mouth, from the coast of Asia towards America, and *neither into* nor *out* of the Strait. These extracts all prove the fact of there being *little* or *no current within* the Strait ; and also, that there was generally very little more outside, or even at the entrance. For the set of 20 miles observed on the 5th of July, though called ' *strong,*' can barely deserve the term ; at all events, it does not convey the idea of a ' violent current rushing in with the greatest velocity.'

" The writer of an article in the Quarterly Review for June last, concludes, (and hypothetically enough) that because there were tides so strong near the Aleutian Islands (at least 5 or 600 miles off) as to run at the rate of seven or eight miles an hour, the water ' must be carried to the northward by these extraordinary tides ;' conceiving that these tides, and the great body of the northern Pacific, which he asserts ' *all navigators have found* to be in motion *towards Behring's Strait,* ' ' are the *strongest* indications of an open and uninterrupted passage for water (uninterrupted *except by ice*) through that strait into the Polar sea ; and a decisive argument

against any such bay as Captain Burney has imagined
to be formed by the junction of the two continents of
Asia and America.'

"That these strong tides, observed among the Aleutian
Islands, extend to the northward as far as Behring's
Strait, seems to be only an *imaginary* assumption, and
till facts have proved that such currents are known to
exist, ' rushing in to the funnel-shaped mouth of the
Strait,' it is unnecessary to reply to the question,
' What becomes of all the water carried to the northward by these extraordinary tides ?' If, indeed, *such*
currents were known to exist, ' rushing in to the funnel-
shaped mouth of the Strait,' they would doubtless occasion a rise and fall, no less remarkable than that which
takes place ' in the Bay of Fundy and the Gulf of
Tonquin.' But facts and experiments having shown
that there is little or no current either within, or outside, near the entrance of Behring's Strait; consequently,
no such effects are produced on the waters *within* the
Strait, for this simple reason—the want of such a cause,
as effects the ' remarkable rise and fall in the Bay of
Fundy and the Gulf of Tonquin.'

" It is therefore needless to have recourse to the chimerical supposition of the existence of a communication,
under the ice, between the Pacific and the Polar sea,
in order to account for the well *authenticated fact*, of
there being little rise or fall of water within Behring's
Strait.

" Besides, *if* the temperature of the water in the Pacific be (as I presume we may conclude it to be) *warmer*
than that within Behring's Strait, it must of course
and necessity flow in (if it does at all) *at the surface*, as
I observed before when treating this subject last February ; and the philosophers of the north have told us

since, in the Edinburgh Review for June last, that 'when water grows warmer it expands, and consequently floats incumbent, communicating afterwards its surplus heat, with extreme slowness, to the mass below.'

"Though such *sage* authority would alone seem sufficient to prove that any *little* current there may be from the Pacific into Behring's Strait, must flow in at the surface (as what little there was *did* in *fact*), and not underneath, it is, however, as well to try how far the philosophers of the south are borne out by *facts*, in asserting so positively that '*all navigators* have found the great body of the northern Pacific to be in motion towards Behring's Strait; and that a current sets in *that* direction along the coast of America on one side, and those of Japan and Kamtschatka on the other.' They acknowledge, however, at the same time, 'that as the observations of the currents on these coasts have been few, and the currents observed might therefore be local and partial, they mean not wholly to rest their argument on them, but to have recourse to other and less equivocal *proofs*, for the *general* movement of the Pacific towards the *north*.' They consider *this* ' to be *indisputably proved* by the immense quantities of drift wood, thrown up on the southern shores of the Aleutian Islands, consisting of fir, larch, aspen, and other trees, the common produce of the two continents of Asia and America.' But as a *proof* of the more southerly parts of the northern Pacific partaking of the same motion, they present to notice ' a curious *fact* mentioned by Stephen Glottof, that among other floating bodies thrown up on the Aleutian Islands, is found the true camphor wood, and another sort, very white, soft, and sweet-scented.'

" Nothing is more possible than that this camphor

wood might come from the Asiatic islands, or some
parts of tropical Asia ; for the south-west monsoon
in the Indian and China seas is known to blow from
May till October, through the sea of Japan, and even
up to the head of the Gulf of Tartary, occasioning
strong currents *to the northward*, and which *might* carry
the camphor wood through the sea of Japan, the Straits
of Matsmai, or Perouse, and among the Kurile Islands ;
from whence a south-west swell, with gales of wind
from that quarter and the southward, might drift it
upon the Aleutian Islands, without *assuming* a conti-
nuation of the general current so much further to the
northward.

"Perouse, after passing Tobaco Xima, about the
end of April, says, ' a strong current *to the northward*
was experienced.' On the 5th of April, near the
Island of Kumi, he found ' the current set to the *northward* with extreme *rapidity.*' When at anchor in the
bay of Ternai, on the 22d of June, he observes, ' The
ebb and flood have no effect upon the direction of the
current half a league in the offing : what we felt at our
anchorage varied only from south-west to south-east,
and its greatest velocity was only a mile an hour.' The
wind was constantly from the southward during his
stay in the Gulf of Tartary, till the 2d of August,
when he sailed from the Bay de Castries.

"After passing the strait which bears his name, we
find no mention of any current to the northward ; but,
on the contrary, on the 10th of August, when off Cape
Crillon, he says, ' We found ourselves a little *to the southward* of our reckoning, but only ten miles.' When near
the Kurile Islands, he remarks, ' Our observations on
the 23d informed us that we had been drifted to the
westward, forty miles in two days ; and we ascertained

the accuracy of these observations on the 24th, by setting the same points we had observed on the 21st, and finding them exactly where they ought to be, according to our longitude observed.' On the 31st he found he had been carried 'ten leagues to the *south-east*.' On his passage from the Kurile Islands to Kamtschatka, *no mention* is made of a current to the *northward*. It appears probable therefore, from the facts stated in the voyage of *this navigator*, that the *northerly* set of current, even *during* the *south-west monsoon*, does not extend further (except in the Gulf of Tartary) than the latitude of 46° or 47° N. And by referring to Clarke's or King's Voyage, we shall find how it set on the east side of Nipon. It is thus described : 'On the 1st of November, at a time when we were 13 leagues to the eastward of White Point, the current set at the rate of *three* miles an hour to the N.E. by N. On the 2d, as we made a nearer approach to the shore, it continued in a similar direction, but was augmented in its rapidity to *five* miles an hour. As we receded from the coast, it again became more moderate, and inclined towards the east. On the 3d, at the distance of 60 leagues from the shore, it set at the rate of three miles an hour to the E.N.E. On the two following days, it turned to the southward, and at 120 leagues from the coast its direction was *south-east*, and its rate did not exceed one mile and a half an hour. It again on the 6th and 7th shifted to the N.E., and its force diminished gradually till the 8th, at which time we could no longer perceive any current.'

" It may therefore be said that the *north-east current* does not *generally* set further to the northward, at any time of the year, in the western part of the northern Pacific, than the parallels of 46° or 47° ; and in all probability not so far.

"On the 2d of July, Captain Krusenstern, when in latitude 34° 3′ N. and longitude 190° 8′ W. says : ' By observation, we found we had been carried by a current 37 miles to the N.E. by N. in the space of three days. On the 29th of June, the last day on which we had observed, the current ran 13 miles to the south.'

"In this part of the Pacific the current may fairly be supposed to be *strongest* in its *northerly* direction *at this season;* because the sun being in that hemisphere, all the winds in the southern Pacific blow from the S.E. ; those in the western and north-western part of that ocean, rounding gradually, in the vicinity of New Holland and New Guinea, to the southward, and S.W. north of the Equator, where they are incorporated with the S.W. monsoon, which then blows from the Indian and China seas. Yet, even here, the current ran at the rate of a little more than half a mile an hour ; and indeed, as it set 'to the *south*,' with a greater velocity, three days before, it may be termed *variable*, rather than '*perpetual.*'

"From the month of September or October, till the month of March, ' the great body of water of the northern Pacific' appears still less likely to be ' in a state of perpetual motion towards Behring's Strait ;' at least all that part of it which is to the northward of 20° N.; because winds more from the N.W. than the S.W. prevail generally quite across the ocean, as far at least to the southward as that latitude. The sun being then in the southern hemisphere, the N.E. trade wind is rarely steady beyond the latitude of 15° or 16° N. in the neighbourhood and westward of the Sandwich Islands ; and, eastward of them, perhaps not so far. In the north-west part of the Pacific the winds in these months (from October till March) are all from the N.E., generally from about the latitude of 40° N. and the coast of Nipon, down to the *Equator*, and the more northerly, as it is approached. And from the Equator to the latitude of at least 16° or 18° S. the N.W. monsoon in this rainy season *there* prevails almost as steady to meridians beyond the Society Islands, as it does from Madagascar to Endeavor Strait.

" Navigators know (or ought to know) that currents depend generally on the direction given to prevalent winds by the power of the sun ; therefore, as the winds in this ocean are locally variable and periodical, though chiefly so to the southward of the Equator, the currents likewise must be periodically changeable, to the northward or southward, though having a *general* tendency to the westward, on both sides the Equator, *at all times ;* but especially north of the Line, as far as the tropic of Cancer ; and such we find to be the case from the testimony of navigators.

" After Perouse quitted Kamtschatka, in the month of October, in running to the eastward, in about the parallel of 37½° N. as far as the longitude of 180°, he experienced strong gales from the south-westward ; and he says, ' the birds appeared to me to come from the south, driven by the violence of the wind ;' and, ' since quitting Kamtschatka we had constantly a very heavy swell : at one time the sea washed away our jolly-boat, which was lashed to the gangway, and we shipped more than a ton of water.'

" Nothing is more possible than that winds like these and a heavy swell would drive the ' camphor wood,' or other floating bodies, upon or even beyond the Aleutian Islands, towards Behring's Strait ; without supposing the existence of a ' perpetual current,' so far in that direction, to account for the fact. And though it is very possible that all the drift wood spoken of 'does not stop at the Aleutian Islands,' and that some, taken up by Captain Clarke in Behring's Strait, might have come from thence; yet, as the Quarterly Reviewers ' have not been able to trace the ' camphor wood' *beyond* the Aleutian Islands,' it is a circumstance rather against, than in favor of, their hypothesis. For as the camphor wood was a floating body too, as well as the other drift wood, and the famous ' *log of mahogany,*' which they traced so marvellous a distance; whatever carried the one, might have carried the other. It is therefore just as possible, that these trees of various kinds, the productions ' of North America, and north, as well as tropical Asia,' may be driven by tides, winds, and swell together, in *all* directions, among the Aleutian Islands, and to the *south*, as well as to the north. And this in fact we find to be the case; for both Captains Cook and Clarke make mention of ' pine trees being driven upon the Sandwich Islands,' which in all probability came from places either to the N.E. or N.W. of those islands.

"Captain Lisianski 'found lying on the beach' of the small island which bears his name, ' several large trunks of trees, the largest of which measured twenty-one feet in circumference at the root; and he says, ' they were like the red-wood tree, that grows on the banks of the Columbia river ' *in America ;*' and *if they* ever grew *there*, they must have had the assistance of a southerly and westerly current to enable them to reach Lisianski Island, in defiance of the *northerly* one, which the Quarterly Reviewers suppose *must* have carried the ' log of mahogany' all the way from the Isthmus of Darien, all along the coast of America, ' through Behring's Strait, and thence along the north coast of

America, and down 'Baffin's Sea' to Disco. But indeed Lisianski, when he passed between Aguian and Tinian on the 16th of November, says, 'From Sitca (on the north-west coast of America) to the Ladrone Islands we had the currents from N.E. to the S.W. The last, which was the strongest, carried us 140 miles to the *southward*, and 200 to the *westward*. Its force was very great near the tropic, but on approaching the Marian Islands it shifted to the westward.' Though this passage is oddly worded, yet it seems to imply that the currents were found to set from the north-east towards the south-west, all the way from Sitca to the Ladrone Islands.

"The Quarterly Reviewers, however, stedfastly believing in the existence of this perpetual current, of their *own creation*, infer that 'logs and trees of the preceding year's drift had passed through the Strait (Behring's) *with the ice* into the 'Polar basin,' and attempt to prove that 'the ice, like the drift wood, has a progressive motion to the northward;' because on the 17th of August Captain Cook fell in with it in lat. 70° 41′ N. and Captain Clarke, 'on the 6th of July following, in 67° N.' Now, as far as I can see, *this* does not seem to prove any thing more than what the facts themselves show—namely, the *different situations* in which the ice was found at two distinct periods in *different* years. It may indeed be presumed, perhaps, that, because Captain Cook fell in with it a month later one year than Captain Clarke did another, the sun's power might have dissolved it further to the northward; or, that the preceding winter might have been less severe, and therefore the ice had not extended so far to the southward. But with respect to the *movement* of the ice *itself*, to the

Data.   H

northward in either year, the *words* of both Captains Cook and Clarke are *expressly* to the *contrary.*

" Captain Cook says, on the 21st of August, ' We were at present in lat. 69° 32' N. and in longitude 195° 48' E., and as the main ice was not far from us, it is evident that it *now covered* a part of the sea, which a few days before had been *free* from it, and that it extended *further towards the south* than where we first fell in with it.' Certainly it did, no less than sixty-nine miles ; for he fell in with it in lat. 70° 41' N.

" Captain Clarke says, in July the following year, ' We had traversed this sea since the 8th of the month, and that, in lines parallel with the course we now steered; the first time, we were unable to penetrate so far north as the second, by eight leagues, and that this last time a compact body of ice had been observed, commonly five leagues *further south* than before. This clearly proves that the vast and solid fields which we saw were decreasing or moveable.' Again, in the year 1778, ' we did not discover the ice till we advanced to the latitude of 70°, on the 17th of August, and we then found it in compact bodies, which extended as far as the eye could reach ; and of which the whole or a part was moveable, since, by its drifting down upon us (from the northward), we narrowly escaped being hemmed in between it and the land.' ' On the 26th of August, in lat. $69\frac{1}{4}$° N. and longitude 184° E., we were obstructed by it in such quantities, that we could not pass either to the north or west. In our second attempt we never had an opportunity of approaching the continent of Asia higher than 67° of latitude, nor that of America in any part, except a few leagues between the latitude 68° and 68° 20' N. But in the last attempt, we were obstructed by it *three degrees further to the southward.*'

" From these passages it is clear, that these navigators
did find the *moveable* ice, in fact, further and further to
the southward, from *some cause*, during the time they,
were among it, in both years. Their judgment on the spot
was, that it moved in *that direction*, and in this they
could not be mistaken with respect to the ice they *saw*
nearest the ships ; for it compelled them to recede from
it further to the southward. *If* it did not move (southward), it must have extended itself, even in these
summer months, by *augmentation*, both in quantity and
superficies, from some (perhaps fixed) mass beyond it
to the northward, which they could not see ; a point
which I shall leave the philosophers of the south to decide for themselves, but which I believe to be most improbable, and those of the north will of course pronounce
impossible : for they have just told us, what I am sure I
little suspected, and I dare say will be no less *surprising* to our arctic navigators when they return, that ' the
fields or shoals of saline ice which during the greater
part of the year cover the arctic seas, are annually
formed and destroyed, and during the thaw, which commonly lasts about three months, the heat of the solar
rays is adequate to the dissolution of *all the ice* produced in the course of the autumn, the winter, and the
spring !!' So that as our polar navigators fortunately
have been in those arctic seas during these ' three
months of thaw,' they will not have been *at all impeded* by ' the fields or shoals of saline ice,' as they are
' *all* thus *annually* formed and *destroyed ;*' but will merely
have to work Tom Cox's Traverse among the icebergs.
And, as the philosophers of the south inform us, that
' the sea through which these massy mountains float,
must be *open*, and where *they* can float a ship will find
no difficulty in sailing,' they must have made great

progress by this time in a navigation *thus cleared* so completely of all obstruction (at least from *ice*), which the ignorant and unlearned among us have foolishly supposed to be the most formidable bar to their success.

" Of course, too, none of the ice seen by Captain Cook and his successors (which the Quarterly Reviewers term ' an impenetrable barrier') could have been of this ' saline' quality ; for when they quitted it, the ice remained nearly in the same state as they found it, undissolved, and apparently undiminished, at the end of the summer. What Captain Cook *saw* on the 17th of August, in lat. 70° 41′ N. is described by him as ' perfectly impenetrable,' and extended from W. by S. to E. by N. as far as the eye could reach. And on the 27th, we are told that ' there being little wind, Captain Cook went in the boat to examine the state of the ice. He found it was as impracticable for ships to pass it as if it had been so many *rocks*. He particularly remarked that it was all pure transparent ice except the upper surface, which was rather porous. It seemed to be composed of frozen snow, and to have been all formed at sea. None of the productions of the land were found incorporated or mixed with it. The Captain judged that the larger pieces reached thirty feet, or more, under water. He thought it highly improbable that this ice could have been the production of the preceding winter ; he was rather inclined to suppose it to have been the production of many winters. It was equally improbable, in his opinion, that the little that now remained of the summer could destroy even the tenth part of what remained of this great mass, for the sun had already exerted upon it the full force and influence of his rays. The sun indeed, according to his judgment, contributes very little towards reducing these enormous masses ;

for though that luminary is above the horizon for a considerable while, it seldom shines out for more than a few hours at a time, and frequently is not seen for several successive days." And I dare say, if poor Captain Cook were alive now, he would still be of the same opinion. Neither would it be in the power of the philosophers of the north to make him believe *that* to be true, which is contrary to the evidence of his senses and experience on the spot. And yet those of the south say, ' it does not appear that Captain Cook entertained any doubt of a passage through Behring's Strait, into the Arctic sea.' I will not venture to say that he did entertain doubt, but I will say that it appears evident, on the face of these extracts, that he could not have entertained the least *hope* of finding any such passage.

"Having thus far disposed of the question of ' a perpetual motion of the great body of the northern Pacific towards Behring's Strait,' 'along the coasts of Japan and Kamstchatka,' let us next see what facts say to its general direction along the west coast of America.— It has been shown that, at the entrance of Behring's Strait, Captains Cook and Clarke found ' very little or no current.' When at anchor near Sledge Island, Captain Cook observes, ' the tide of flood came from the eastward, and set to the westward, till between the hours of ten and eleven o'clock ; from which time, till two o'clock in the morning, the stream set to the eastward, and the water fell three feet: the flood running both stronger and longer than the ebb, we concluded there was a *westerly* current, besides the tide.' Further to the southward, off Shoalness, he remarks that ' the tide of flood set to the north, and the ebb to the southward,' 'and among the Aleutian Islands the tides were strong and regular.' The general set was W.S.W., and E.N.E., clear of them; and various among them, according to the directions of the channels. Subsequent navigators appear to have found them the same, not only there, but every where else (though setting in directions according to localities), all along the N.W. coast of America, *from* these Islands as far down to the southward as 40° of latitude. Nor do any of the navigators on that coast (as far I find) mention the prevalence of a *northerly* current at any time of the year.

" On the 11th of October, the day Captain Vancouver sailed from Nootka Sound for Monterey, he says, ' when in 100 fathoms water, by the lead when on the ground, the vessel seemed to lie as if at anchor.' So that there was *no* current at all here at that time, and little or none seems to have been observed all the way down to Monterey. After quitting that port on the 2nd of December, he observes, on passing the Island of Guadaloupe on the 8th, ' The observation made on that and the preceding day exactly agreed with the ship's run by log.' On the 23rd of December, when in lat. 13° 50′ N. and longitude 100° 55′ W., Captain Vancouver says, ' During our passage thus far from Monterey, it did not appear that we had been much affected by currents ; the log and observations having agreed very nearly, and the difference between the longitude by dead reckoning and that which I considered to be the true longitude, had not exceeded half a degree ; the dead reckoning having been in general to the eastward of the truth. The wind in the north-western quarter continued to blow a steady breeze, and as we advanced to the south-eastward increased in force.' ' From this position, the current set towards the south and east, and sometimes to the northward of east (occasioned no doubt by an indraught towards the Gulf of Panama), particularly near the Island of Cocos, and from thence to the Galepagos Islands ; but after passing *them*, the currents shifted, and ran to the southward, and to the westward. I have been tempted to accompany Captain Vancouver thus far down the coast, to try to discover, if possible, that current on whose *supposed existence* the philosophers of the south ground their extraordinary conclusion that the mahogany plank which the Governor of Disco's table was made of, and also a tree of logwood found there, ' could only have reached the spot on which they were found, along the coast of America from the Isthmus of Darien.' *How* they got there, God only knows ! But if Captain Vancouver's account of the currents he met with along that coast are to be credited, it is impossible they could have gone thither by the route supposed, or ever have reached Behring's Strait ; even admitting it possible that these logs had been drifted from the Gulf of Panama by the equatorial current, quite across the Pacific, and afterwards driven all the way up to the northward along the coasts of Nipon and Kamtschatka. Indeed it seems much more possible, and probable too, that these very logs of mahogany found their way to Disco somehow or other from the Gulf of Mexico. It is very clear that the gulf-stream might have carried them up to, or perhaps beyond Newfoundland, from whence, it is not impossible that by other currents or local tides they might have got into eddies close in along the coast of Labrador, and even into Hudson's Bay, and out again through some of the openings furthest to the northward, and so across Davis's Strait to Disco. *They* might also, as well as the other log of mahogany ' picked up by Admiral Lewenorne,' have been driven from some part of the northern Atlantic, by southerly gales, and heavy seas. For, floating at the *surface*, they would not feel the influence *there* of the perpetual *underflow* from the north, which brings the icebergs down to the southward, against the heaviest gales, because they are deeply immersed in it. And if thus driven near the S.W. part of Greenland, they might be carried by the eddy and regular tides which have been observed on the west side of it.

" But even admitting the possibility of these logs entering Behring's Strait by the *marvellous* long route supposed, another obstacle perhaps lies in the way of our belief of their reaching Disco from thence. It is true, the philosophers of the south have cleared the way for them at once, by *assuming* as a fact without sufficient evidence, that Davis's Strait *is open* to the northward *because* it has been *stated* that ' a perpetual current runs there to the southward ; sometimes with a velocity of four or even of five miles an hour.' This may be so: but I apprehend that well-established fact and experiment will prove this statement *not* to be *quite correct*. Nor will any seamen who know what a current of five knots is, believe that *such* a current *can* exist where whale ships can keep on their fishing ground for weeks together, without the least difficulty. But, as I observed before on this subject last February, it is highly probable, that either from the interruption of *lands*, or shoals, between Greenland and America, a comparatively small quantity of current passes from the ' Polar basin,' through Davis's Strait, and that much of the ice, as well as the current, may have Hudson's Bay for its origin.

" I shall only add here, what the philosophers of the

north say to Davis's Strait being open, or closed by land to the north. They are of opinion that 'Baffin's last voyage showed that Davis's Strait is absolutely shut all along the north side ; and proved that either no passage exists on its western coast, or none which is for the shortest time of the year practicable ;' thus leaving the poor 'log of mahogany' no *chance* of having reached Disco that way, from Behring's Strait.

" The 3d peculiarity mentioned by Captain Burney was, that ' the bottom not being swept by streams, was of soft ooze ;' and in Clarke's Voyage we read, that ' the bottom towards the middle was of soft slimy mud ; and near either shore, a brownish sand intermixed with a few shells and small fragments of bones.'

" With regard to this fact, it is however sufficient to observe, that perhaps few seamen who have had much experience of tides and currents in soundings, will consider a bottom of ooze or slime as any *proof* of its *not* being swept by streams ; or admit that a bottom, over which the strongest tide or current runs, *must therefore* be stony, sandy, or gravelly; for they cannot but be acquainted with many examples to the contrary. One of the most remarkable that occurs to my recollection just now, is the Gulf of Martaban ; in which the almost entire bottom is composed of the softest slimy mud, though tides at the springs run at the rate of 7 or 8 knots an hour.

" The 4th and last peculiarity noticed by Captain Burney, and perhaps the strongest of all, is, that ' the soundings were observed to decrease to the northward beyond the latitude of 68° 45′ N.' The Quarterly Reviewers have endeavored to prove the contrary, though perhaps not satisfactorily ; at least not according to my apprehension of Captain Burney's meaning. Both

Data.   I

he and they must be near the truth, as it lies somewhere between them, in the small space of 12 feet only.
The fact is, the bottom is not *very* uneven where the
soundings vary only a fathom or two in as many leagues;
and in this place they were certainly very regular.

"When Captain Burney says, that 'in steering to
the westward, they did not find the depth to increase,'
he seems clearly to mean, when at a considerable distance from the land, towards mid-channel. And when
Captain Cook 'states distinctly,' that in approaching
the American coast ' the water shoaled gradually;' and
when he was obliged to anchor in 6 fathoms, it was
found that the water shoaled gradually towards the
land, ' he as clearly alludes to soundings very near
the land of America. And again, when in 6 fathoms,
he says, ' as we advanced to the westward the soundings deepened,' (as of course they must to mid-channel,
where the depth is 28 and 30 fathoms,) it does not at all
bear upon the question of there being more or less water
generally from *south* to *north*, on which the Quarterly
Reviewers are at issue with Captain Burney. That the
depth of water midway between Asia and America
was about 29 or 30 fathoms, and, as Captains Clarke
and Gore state, 'decreasing gradually as we approached
either continent,' (traversing on a parallel,) is very true.
But how can this affect Captain Burney's statement
of the fact of the general depth being less to the northward? Though in *some particular* spots to the northward of 68° 45', a little more water was perhaps found,
yet still the *general* depth might certainly have been
less. And as Captain Burney judged on the spot, from
various circumstances, as well as *all* the soundings at
the time, *his* opinion on that matter is certainly more
likely to be correct, than one formed from the perusal

of journals, where most probably all the soundings are not inserted ; or the examination of charts, where still fewer may be laid down.

"Upon the whole, then, taking it for granted that the 4th and last fact is established, or at least, if there is *not less*, there certainly is nearly the *same* depth, as far as the ships advanced to the northward, in Behring's Strait ; let us now inquire how far the peculiarities observed by Captain Burney warrant the supposition of the junction of the two continents, even admitting that the soundings did positively decrease to the northward.

" Captain Burney grounds his supposition chiefly, if not entirely, on these peculiarities ; and the philosophers of the north, after enumerating them, conclude their article in these words :—' These are obviously distinct indications of an inclosed sea.'

" But it *may* be inclosed *without* the existence of any land *between* Asia and America ; for as to the fact of the depth of water decreasing to the northward, *that* cannot be admitted as proof of there *being land* in that direction connecting the two continents ; because the very same decrease would take place upon the acclivity of a bank extending east and west, whose shoalest part might be at, or near the surface at some, yet undefined, distance to the northward, beyond where the ships advanced ; and thence deepening again, probably as gradually, to the north. And when two different facts *may* result from circumstances in all respects not exactly alike, the supposition of one or the other is equally well bottomed. If such a bank exist near the surface, it would doubtless occasion peculiarities the very same as those observed ; and if there be such a bank at some depth under the surface ; or even, if the depth of 30 fathoms or more continue, as is most probable, far beyond the parallel reached by Captain Cook, there is much reason (and fact too) to conclude, (as I have observed before on this subject,) that the *ice itself* must as completely inclose an expanse beyond Behring's Strait, so long as Nature holds her course, as land itself would ; and consequently all the peculiarities observed by Captain Burney must, on that account, equally exist.

" In attempting to prove this inclosure by ice, I shall argue chiefly from the *facts, stated* and agreed in, and therefore, it is presumed, accredited fully by both parties of philosophers.

" Those of the south have informed us, that 'icebergs or mountains of ice are generated on the land, either in valleys, or against steep shores:' and those of the north agreeing on this point, minutely describe the process of their formation, and consider them to be the gradual production of perhaps 'many centuries,' and ' the accumulation of ages.'

" The philosophers of the south have named New Siberia as ' the probable source of the icebergs which come down Davis's Strait, through which they assume ' an uninterrupted communication' with the Polar basin. But those of the north believing that Baffin's last voyage ' showed that Davis's Strait is absolutely shut all along the north side,' it is inferred, I presume, by them, that the icebergs ' which appear most frequently in Davis's Strait, all originate there, particularly along the western coast of Greenland, ' from whence every year, but especially in hot seasons, they are partially detached from their seats, and whelmed into the deep sea.' Now on this joint doctrine of both parties, as to the *formation* of icebergs in valleys, and against steep shores ; as the Arctic sea is bounded *chiefly* by the coasts of Siberia and America, where there perhaps *may* be ' valleys and steep shores,' it may be presumed that icebergs must be produced there also, as well as at New Siberia, in Baffin's Bay, and on the west side of Greenland. And as the remarkable fact, stated by one party, that *all* the ice brought by the S.W. current round Spitzbergen is *field ice*, is not denied by the other, (for indeed *they* say that icebergs are seen floating *only* in Davis's Strait,) a question arises; viz. If it may be allowed probable, or even possible, on *these* grounds, that icebergs may also be formed on some parts of the lands extending from Nova Zembla eastward to Greenland, pray what becomes of them, if they cannot pass through Davis's Strait, and be not brought by the south-west current round Spitzbergen, and be very seldom met with in the eastern Greenland sea?

" Not being composed of that saline ice, which we are told ' is annually formed and destroyed,' they must remain, and drive about in all directions, as long as they have sufficient depth of water to float in, *not* till they 'are divided, scattered and dissipated,' as ' the shoals of ice in the Arctic seas commonly are, before the end of June, nor till they are dissolved. For one party tells ' how little the influence of an Arctic summer is, even, on fields of ice, perpetually surrounded as they are by a freezing atmosphere created by themselves.' On their hypothesis therefore it is evident, that as *part* of these immense masses must remain at the end of the summer, to *that* part the ensuing winter must add something. When speaking on this subject on a former occasion, I supposed it probable that the process of *melting* and *freezing* may be going on in the Arctic regions on the same body of ice (if of a magnitude to be sufficiently immersed) at the same time; and perhaps in winter, as well as in summer, owing to the *increasing* temperature of the water from the surface downwards in proportion (perhaps) to its depth. The philosophers of the north have *since* ' demonstrated that the Polar seas are always ready, under the action of any frosty wind, to suffer congelation; and though the annual variations of the weather are in these seas expended on the superficial waters, without disturbing the vast abyss below ;' yet as the water drawn up from a considerable depth *is warmer*, within the Arctic circle than what lies on the surface, the floating ice, accordingly, begins to melt ' generally on the *under side*, from the slow communication of the heat sent upwards.' Though we are told, ' that before the end of June the shoals of ice in the Arctic seas are commonly divided, scattered and dissipated, and a few weeks are commonly sufficient to dissolve the floating ice ;' and though ' during the thaw, which commonly lasts about three months, the heat of the solar rays is adequate to the dissolution of *all* the ice produced in the course of the autumn, the winter and the spring ! !' yet it is to be presumed that the *icebergs* are not meant to be included in this ' all.' Indeed it is observed, that ' some of them are 2000 feet high ;' and, supposing the surface of the sea to be at 52°, (which I dare say it never was, nor ever will be in the Arctic seas,) an iceberg having only 600 feet elevation would require one hundred and fifty days for its dissolution, and double that time, if the temperature of the sea it floats in should be at 42°. Even at this rate it cannot dissolve, for it would require at least ten months. But being indeed informed further, that ' within the Arctic circle, the *surface* of the ocean, being never much warmer than about the 27° of Fahrenheit's scale, is, in the decline of summer, soon cooled down to the limit at which congelation commences,' it seems that even such an iceberg could NEVER be dissolved there.

"And as 'in the space of a few weeks only, visited by the slanting and enfeebled rays, frost resumes its tremendous sway, and it begins to snow as early as August,' the conclusion (at least on *such* data) seems evident, that icebergs even while they float within 'the Polar basin,' and can find no passage thence into a warmer temperature, are more likely to augment their bulk, by the effect of frost, snow, and hail *above*, than to be diminished below the surface of the sea. This increase will be much greater still on such icebergs as may take the ground, on the *bank* if there be one, but if there be not, in the shoal water (which is very insufficient to float them) extending from Asia to America; for the temperature of the water being of course colder there, the effect of dissolution under the surface will be greatly diminished ; whilst the augmentation above will be the same as if it floated. So that every fall of snow and hail, adding to masses of ice thus situated, *must* form, collectively, one ' impenetrable barrier,' as Captain Cook termed what he saw. A barrier that doubtless has been, and will remain *there* for ages, fixed to the bottom by its own inertia, extending probably compact and immoveable far to the northward of the parallel reached by Cook ; and perhaps rising in mountains, as far as soundings extend, and thence declining towards its margin, which may be subject to continual disruption, by the swell of the sea in deeper water : or, it may present to the north a rugged perpendicular front, bidding stern defiance to the roaring of the winds or the raging billows of the sea, and mocking the vain attempts of man to pass it.

" That there must exist such a barrier as this, inclos-
ing an expanse to the.*northward* of Behring's Strait (*if*
there be no land there), appears to me to be little
less than certain, and which must be kept still more
compact, along its northern boundary, by the constant
pressure against it of the Polar stream from the north,
which I have supposed on a former examination of this
subject, and which therefore can find no egress from the
Polar sea, down to the regions of equatorial heat,
except to the eastward of Greenland and Spitzbergen.

" Another circumstance, amounting almost to a proof
of the passage by Behring's Strait being closed up, even
against fish of large size, much more against *ships*, is,
that none of our navigators (at least as far as I know)
have mentioned seeing a single whale within the Strait,
where the water is not deep, and the ice abundant. It
of course does not follow, that because they *saw* none,
there were *not* any ; yet if there had been any, it is
more than probable that our navigators would have
seen some of them during their stay there. And the
philosophers of the south remark, ' that whales are generally found in those parts of the Arctic seas where ice
most abounds, and where it has taken the ground on
shores and banks.' They have also mentioned a ' circumstance of whales struck with harpoons in the sea
of Spitzbergen or in Davis's Strait, being found on the
north-west coast of America !' *They* consider *this* as
affording an additional argument for a *free* communication between the Atlantic and Pacific, by way of
Behring's Strait.

" Though I have endeavored to prove that an expanse to the northward of Behring's Strait is thus perpetually inclosed by a conglobation of icebergs, on the
supposition of their formation on other lands surround-

ing the Polar sea, as well as at New Siberia and in
Davis's Straits ; yet even allowing that this supposition,
on the ground it rests, is *improbable,* and admitting that
none of *these* stupendous masses *are* so formed, but only
such ice as Captain Cook *saw,* whatever might be its
quality or kind ; yet it seems to me no less clear, that
even ice of that kind, collected as it is between two
lands, must by its annual augmentation have formed an
equally ' impenetrable barrier: ' for what our navigators saw was evidently as abundant at the close of each
summer as they found it on their first arrival among it.
This fact shows that ' *all* the ice produced *there* in the
winter, the autumn, and the spring, is *not* dissolved,'
nor even ' dissipated,' though ' divided and scattered.'
Therefore, the quantity dissolved each summer being
evidently *less, generally,* than what is ' produced in the
autumn, the winter, and the spring,' the consequence
must be (by congelation at least) an *increase* on the
whole of that solid mass further to the northward, which
I presume is immoveably fixed on the bottom. It is very
true, that much of the ice along the *southern* margin may
be partially dissolved by the rays of the summer sun ;
and being subject to disruption by the motion of the sea,
in gales of wind (from the southward), may therefore
move about in an extent of many leagues to the southward of the main body, as our navigators found it did.

" Much of the ice may be of that saline quality which
is said to be ' annually formed and destroyed,' but the
greatest part of what Cook saw *was not ;* for he says, ' it
seemed to be wholly composed of frozen snow.' In
another place he says, on the 17th of August, when in
lat. 70° 41' N. ' We were at present close to the edge of
the ice, which was as compact as a wall, and appeared
to be at least 12 feet high ;' Captain Cook particularly

remarked, that the ice was all *pure* and *transparent*, except the upper surface, which was rather ' porous.' And as the philosophers of the north have assured us, that *pure transparent* ice projects one tenth, as it swims in the sea, even this part of the ice must have been immersed to within 12 fathoms of the bottom : but Cook observes, ' further to the northward it seemed to be *much higher ;*' and in all human probability, the ice at no great distance to the northward, beyond what he saw, was immoveably fixed at the bottom, and continued so *as far as soundings extend.* For it is mentioned in Clarke's Voyage, that the height of the highest ice they saw ' was estimated at 16 or 18 feet,' which therefore must have been immersed to within two or three fathoms of the bottom, according to the soundings they had at the time.

"It is also worthy of remark, that the water was found to be somewhat shallower on the coast of America than that of Asia, at an equal distance ; our navigators were therefore able to penetrate near three degrees further to the northward, on the side of America, ' because they came up with the ice in both years sooner, and in larger quantities, on the coast of Asia.' This strong fact seems of itself almost sufficient to prove, that the heavy ice further to the northward must have been aground in some depth ; for if it were all water-borne, and moveable, as the ice was which our navigators saw nearest the ships, why should it not move as far to the southward on one coast, as it did on the other, so long as it could float? The only reason can be, because its progress in that direction was sooner stopped, by the bottom being nearer the surface on the coast of America, than it was on that of Asia, and consequently giving to the main body of *fixed* ice, a general direction of about E.N.E. and

W.S.W., according to the probable line of equal depth of water.

"Whether this barrier may at any time of the year reach as far as to the Pole itself, is a question I have offered my surmises on before, regarding the winter ; and I agreed in opinion with the philosophers of the south, that the sea *will be* (*I* only say *may be*) there found free from ice in the summer ; ' presuming that there is proba‑ bly a warmer summer temperature to dissolve it at the Pole itself, than any where else, to the southward of it, as far as 75° or 80°; because, when the sun's rays first strike the Pole, they will be felt there incessantly for six months ; but with what force and effect I had then to learn. For this information we are now, however, indebted to the philosophers of the north. They assure us, that 'it may be shown that, under the Pole, the action of the solar light is, at the time of the solstice, one-fourth part greater than at the Equator, and sufficient in the course of a day to melt a sheet of ice *one inch and a half* thick.' They further inform us, that ' it may be *proved by experiment*, that, under the Pole itself, the power of the sun at the solstice could, in the space of a week, melt a stratum of five inches of ice. We may hence fairly compute the *annual* effect to be sufficient for thawing to the depth of *forty inches.* It should likewise be observed, that owing to the ha‑ ziness of the atmosphere in the northern latitudes, those singular emanations, which are now found al‑ ways to dart from an azure sky, and in the more tempe‑ rate climates to diminish the calorific action of the sun, often by one-fifth part, can scarcely exist. On this account, perhaps, the estimate of the annual destruction of the polar ice may be swelled to the thickness of four feet.'

" There appears to be some mistake or discordance in this computation ; for, in the first case, as ' the solar light can be shown to be sufficient in the course of a day to melt a sheet of ice of an inch and a half thick,' it could in the space of a week melt a stratum of *ten inches and a half,* instead of ' *five :*' and by the same rule the annual effect may be sufficient for thawing to the depth of *eighty-four inches and a half,* instead of ' *forty ;*' or perhaps the estimate of the annual destruction of polar ice may be swelled to more than *eight feet* instead of ' four.' If, on the other hand, it be allowed, that only ' five inches' are melted in the space of a week, there cannot be *so much* as an inch and a half melted in the course of a day, as is stated in the first case.

" Whether either of these *computations* will be '*proved*' to be correct by the *experiments* Captain Buchan is gone to make in that quarter this year of our Lord, God knows ; but, *if* he should have proceeded *between Greenland and Spitzbergen, I fear not ;* for the route to be pursued towards the Pole with most *probability* of success, must doubtless be midway *between Spitzbergen and Nova Zembla,* for the reasons I have before given. Even the philosophers of the south acknowledge that ' the lands are usually surrounded with ice,' and therefore recommend that ' ships, instead of coming *near the land,* and endeavouring to pass through *narrow straits,*' ought to avoid the land, and keep as ' much as possible in the *open sea,* and in or near the edge of the current, where the sea may be expected to be free.' Those of the north indeed go still further, and tell us, that a ' few weeks are commonly sufficient to disperse and dissolve the floating ice, and the sea is at last *open* for a short and dubious interval to the pursuits of the adventurous mariner.' *Their* opinion as to the practicability of reaching the Pole seems, upon the whole, rather slender; though not that it is impossible: for though they say, ' as the cold increases but very little in advancing to the higher latitudes, the vast expanse of ice which covers the Polar basin may be nearly dissolved at the close of every summer; and *if* the intrepid navigator, therefore, could seize the short and *quivering* interval, he might push on to the Pole itself;' yet ' they consider the scheme of penetrating to the Pole itself as *more daring*' than ' the project of finding a N.W. passage to China; which *they must* at the same time suppose to be *impossible*, if they believe that the peculiarities observed by Captain Burney *are*, as they assert, ' obviously indications of an *inclosed sea.*'' Of the success of either plan *their* hopes are confessed to be ' extremely slender;' but the ground they have taken leaves them in fact as much without any *hope* at all, as I confess I am, of success.

" There is another point on which these men of science and learning differ so materially, that those who have read one review, and perhaps felt disposed to pin their faith upon it, without much consideration, are astonished, on perusing the other, to find almost every thing denied, or apparently refuted; leaving them just as wise as they were before, or perhaps still worse, in a state of indecision and doubt between both, or with no opinion at all. The question I mean is, whether the remarked chilliness of our climate in the years 1816 and 17 was in any degree owing to the influence of icebergs passing in the Atlantic, which there has been so much *talk* about? The philosophers of the south say, ' it would be a waste of words to enter into any discussion on the diminution of temperature, which must necessarily be occasioned by the proximity of large mountains and islands of ice ; and therefore it is equally clear, that our climate must have been affected by the vast accumulation of ice on the east coast of Greenland. It can scarcely be doubted, therefore, that the remarkable chilliness of the atmosphere, in the summer months of 1816 and 1817, was owing to the appearance of ice in the Atlantic.'

" Now my own sensations assure me, that a northerly wind is *cold*, and the thermometer that they have not deceived me. I also suppose this wind to be cold here, because it comes from regions where ice is known to abound. And if there were *as much* ice due west of us, and the wind came from it towards us, I dare say the atmosphere under the lee of it would be chilled by it to a certain degree, according to the distance from it ; but how much and how far, I shall leave to the philosophers of the *north* to ' *compute*.' Though these philosophers deny all this, yet at the same time they seem to me to acknowledge it.

" After most ably explaining the ' true principles which regulate the distribution of heat over the globe, independent of every hypothesis, by the direct appeal to experiment and observation,' they assure us, that ' whatever may be the vicissitudes of the Polar ice, they cannot in any sensible manner affect the climates of the lower latitudes ;' that ' the idea is quite chimerical that any winds could ever transport the Polar influence to our shores.' Some persons ' have imagined that the mountains or islands of ice which are occasionally drifted into the Atlantic ocean must be sufficient by their frigorific influence to modify the character of our climate ; but a little reflection will convince us that

such remote influence on our climate must be quite in-
significant.'

" After enlarging at length, and with great ingenuity,
they remark, that ' the three last seasons, which have
been reckoned very open, have succeeded to winters
notoriously cold and protracted ; for *our severe* winters
are *occasioned* by the prevalence of *northerly* winds,
which *must* arrive at the Polar sea *from the south*, and
consequently transport so much warmth as may check
the usual rigor of the frost ! !'

" Now, though it is possible that these northerly
winds *might* have come all the way from the Pacific
ocean, and 'have transported so much warmth as
might check the usual rigor of the frost,' yet it by no
means follows of course that they *must ;* or that *our*
northerly winds were ever entitled, by having traversed
so extensive a track, to the denomination of *south.*
For it is just as possible, and much more probable, that
these northerly winds originated and commenced their
journey somewhere in our hemisphere on this side the
Pole.   But whether they did, or did not, come all the
way from the Pacific, as southerly winds, to the Pole,
whence they became *northerly as to us* here, it is, however,
clearly, though perhaps inadvertently, *admitted* by these
philosophers, that these said northerly winds had positively acquired a frigorific ' character,' somewhere, and
somehow, *on the passage* to our 'lower latitudes.'   For
it is acknowledged that ' *their* prevalence *occasioned* (on
account of their ' frigorific influence' it may be supposed)
our '*severe winters :*' an acknowledgment apparently
at variance with the former opinion, that ' whatever may
be the vicissitudes of the Polar ice, they cannot in any
sensible manner affect the climates of the lower latitudes ;' and that ' the idea is quite chimerical, that *any*

winds could ever transport the Polar influence to our shores.'

" These northern philosophers have satisfactorily explained the true principles which regulate the distribution of heat over the globe, particularly regarding the temperature of the earth, at certain depths. But in applying these principles to the temperature of the sea, some of the conclusions appear not so well to accord with experiment and observation. They say, that ' in the more temperate regions of the globe, the superficial waters of lakes and seas, as they grow warmer, and therefore specifically lighter, still remain suspended by their acquired buoyancy; but whenever they come to be chilled, they suffer contraction, and are precipitated ; hence the deep water of lakes and seas is *always* considerably *colder* than what floats at the surface.' [Query, —Would not the deep water of a *frozen* lake or sea in the more temperate regions be warmer than at the surface, for the same reason that it is so in Polar regions ?] It is then said, that ' the gradation of cold is distinctly traced to the depth of 20 fathoms, *below which* the diminished temperature continues nearly *uniform*, as far as the sounding line can reach.'

" Though the sea, as well as the land, may have its isothermal lines, yet at what various depths, according to the temperature of the atmosphere, climates, and other mutable circumstances, has not yet been discovered; but certainly generally *far below* the depth of *twenty fathoms*. For it would seem that there must be at the surface, on two parallels, somewhere between the Equator and the Poles, two stations, or points, *not fixed*, but *changeable*, and *dependent* on the *atmospheric temperature* over them : between which stations, or points, and the *Equator*, the water will be progressively colder, in proportion perhaps to its depth ; and between each, and its respective *Pole*, the water will be warmer in proportion perhaps to its depth from the surface. But this *general* rule will not, of course always hold good, where there are *soundings*, or in confined waters near land.

" The following experiments will prove that between the tropics, and in the temperate zones at sea, when the temperature of the atmosphere exceeds that of the surface of the sea, the superficial water is generally warmer than that at certain depths beneath it (I say *generally*, because in soundings and confined waters local causes may effect many exceptions to this rule), and in all probability, the greater the depth the colder the fluid in *that* case.

" On the 23d of Feb., in lat. 52° S. and about the longitude of 50° W., Captain Krusenstern says the temperature of the air was 12° Reaumur, of the surface 10°, and at the depth of 55 fathoms 8½°; the whole depth at the time being 75 fathoms.—On the 9th of March, in lat. 50° 20′ S. and longitude 72° 45′ W. the temperature of the air was 4° R., the surface 2½° ; at the depth of 60 fathoms 2½° ; and at 100 fathoms 1½°.—On the 24th of May, 56 miles south of the Equator, and in longitude 146° 16′ W. the temperature of the air and surface were equal at 22¼° ; and at the depth of 100 fathoms 12½°. On the 22d of June, on the tropic of Cancer, in the Pacific, the temperature of the surface was 20° 5′ R. ; at the depth of 25 fathoms 19° 5′ ; at 50 fathoms 17° 2′ ; and at 125 fathoms 13° 3′ ; so that there was a progressive decrease of temperature of 1° in 25 fathoms ; 3° 3′ in 50 fathoms, and 7° 2′ at 125 fathoms. Many more examples might be given to the same effect, if it were necessary. One very remarkable one is mentioned by

Data. L

Mr. Clarke Abel in his recent work. He informs us that Captain Wauchope of H. M. S. Eurydice, when within a few leagues of the Equator, put his apparatus overboard, and allowed it to descend till it had run out 1400 fathoms of line, but he estimated the perpendicular depth at 1000 fathoms. The temperature of the surface was 73°. On drawing up the instrument, he found the thermometer marking 42°; a difference of temperature of 31°. And there can be no doubt but that the difference of the temperature was progressive from the surface down to that depth.

"The philosophers of the north observe : ' That in shallow seas, the cold substratum of liquid is brought nearer to the surface ;' but though as a general axiom this may be true, yet it may not be relied on in particular cases, much less ' that the increasing coldness of the water drawn up from only the depth of a few fathoms, may therefore indicate to the navigator who traverses the wide ocean, his approach to banks or land.' Indeed no navigator who has had any experience in the matter would, I apprehend, place the least dependence on so precarious a guide ; for he must know that many experiments would show its fallibility.

" Some instances, in proof of this, may be collected from the journal of Captain Hall of the Lyra, lately published, who made some experiments on the temperature of the surface near the Loochoo Islands, and in the Yellow Sea.

" On the 19th of July, when off Chusan in, 32 fathoms water, the temperature of the surface of the sea was 78° and 80° ; and on the 22d, in 43 fathoms, it was only 77° and 72° ; but when at anchor in 3½ fathoms, in the Gulf of Peecheelee, in latitude 38° 42′ N., and longitude 117° 49′ W., on the 27th of July, the temperature of the surface was as high as 82°. Also on the 3d of August, when at anchor off Peiho, the surface was 82° at noon, and 80° at midnight, and *there* it was generally *warmer* than the atmosphere itself. When at anchor in Napakiang harbour, the general temperature of the surface of the sea was about 83°, but out at sea, off the Island of Loochoo, when in latitude 26° 36′ N. and longitude 127° 56′ W. the surface was 4 or 5 degrees *colder*, being on the 14th and 15th only 79½° and 78°. Again, on the 20th of October, at anchor in Napakiang harbour, when the autumnal cold had lowered the temperature of the sea's surface *there* to 75½° and 75°, (or 7 or 8 degrees *below* what it was when anchored there before) yet in the Japan *sea* the surface was also lower, being 74° and 73°. Thus in these particular instances, the water became warmer (at the surface at least) the *nearer* the land was approached, and also as the depth of water *decreased*.

" Mr. Clarke Abel has also published the result of a few experiments made by him on the temperature of the sea, *in soundings*, both at the surface and bottom, which, though useful and satisfactory, are not conclusive. They are shown in the following table.

Date.	North Latitude.	East Longitude.	Depth, Fathoms.	Place.	Tempe-rature.			Difference of Temperature		
					Air.	Surface.	Bottom.	Of the Air and Surface.	Of the Surface and Bottom.	Of the Air and Bottom.
No July 1816.	° ′	° ′			°	°	°	°	°	°
1 23 8 A.M.	35 01	123 46	40	Open Sea.	76	74	65	2	9	11
2 24 Noon	36 24	122 59	15	do.	75	71	67	4	4	8
3 25 8 A.M.	37 30	122 40	20	do.	72	67	62	5	5	10
4 8 P.M.			15	do.	74	69	66	7	3	8
5 26 6 A.M.	37 58	121 34	15	Amongst the Meetaw Islands.	74	67	66	7	1	8
6 27 11 P.M.	38 12	120 30	15	Gulf of Pee-cheelee.	75	74	72	1	2	3

" From these experiments (Mr. Clarke Abel observes)
it appears : ' 1st. That the sea diminishes in its temperature in proportion to its depth.' ' 2d. That the
difference of the temperature of the surface and any
given depth, within a certain range, is *greater at sea*
than *near* the land.' ' 3d. That the difference of the
temperature at the surface and bottom is *greatest* when
that of the air and surface is *least.*'

" The 1st and 3d positions appear evident on the
face of the experiments, but the experiment No. 3
seems to affect the correctness of the 2d position ; for
the difference of the surface, and 20 fathoms depth,
was 5 degrees, and by that of the 1st experiment, made
further from the land, there was a difference of 9° only
in 40 fathoms ; which was *less* in proportion than near
the land. It is remarkable, however, that all these
experiments (except the 3d) prove, as far as they go,
that in the depth of 15 fathoms the water at the bottom
was invariably warmer, than it was found to be at the
depth of 40 fathoms 'in the open sea ;' and in the
Gulf of Peecheelee, where the 6th experiment was
made, it was no less than 7° degrees warmer at the
depth of 15 fathoms.

" The lower state of the atmosphere when the 3d
experiment was made, would seem to account for the
temperature of the water at the bottom being so much
below what it was found to be by the others.

" There is also a much greater proportional difference
of the temperature of the air and water at the depth of
20 fathoms, than there was by the rest of the experiments.

" These experiments also prove, that in these ' shallow seas,' however, the cold substratum of liquid, *was
not* brought nearer the surface, at this season of the

year ; so that in these instances, there was *no* increasing ' coldness of water drawn up from the depth of only a few fathoms, to indicate to the navigator, who traverses the wide ocean, his approach to land or banks ;' but the reverse.

"After this digression from the chief point of my inquiry, I shall now conclude, by merely observing, that as the success or failure of both expeditions ultimately depends upon there being a passage (*practicable for ships*) or no passage, from ' the Polar Basin' into the Pacific,—a point, on which so much has been said and written by philosophers—on which scarcely two persons are found to agree—all have their doubts, and none have any positive knowledge,—it would really seem that *this*, of all others, from its superior importance, ought to have been first determined, and not left as the *last*, and in all human probability the most difficult to be solved by our Polar navigators. And that too (if ever they reach so far) near the long-hoped for close of a toilsome voyage, when they may be reduced by sickness or deaths ; or at least so worn down by anxiety and fatigue, as to be unable to return the way they came, or to surmount the difficulties opposed to their further progress.

" The despatching these expeditions by the way they are gone, to explore a passage through Behring's Strait, seems as if a person were ordered to enter a certain labyrinth, by a well known passage on one side, but to pass out of it on the opposite by another, which one half the world *supposed* there might be, and the other half that there might not—of whose existence *most* were in doubt, and none knew any thing, except a few, who had twice tried, but could find no passage beyond a certain barrier which *they* found to be *insurmountable*.

" Now if this very barrier should happen to be generally considered as the probably chief obstacle to be surmounted, and could, without much difficulty, be approached from the side where it lay ; certainly the most rational, the most prudent and advisable course should seem to be, first of all to have this barrier examined on *that* side, and its nature and extent fully ascertained, before the person be sent on what people of common sense would perhaps call ' a wild-goose-chase,' without such information.

" However, though *this part* of the expeditions may fail, yet if our navigators return, let them have reached where they may, they will at least bring back with them more correct hydrographical information than any we can have at present. And in all probability the observations they may have been enabled to make in the Arctic regions will enlarge the bounds of science ; and for that alone, though no other benefit should be derived from them, it was highly befitting a country like this to send them out."

In the month of October, 1818, the Dorothea and Trent arrived, after the most strenuous, but unsuccessful endeavors to penetrate towards the North Pole, *between* Greenland and Spitzbergen. The Isabella and Alexander also returned to Deptford on the 21st of November ; and in the beginning of the following year Captain Ross published an account of his voyage. A writer in the Quarterly Review, No. 41, published in May 1819, in criticising that work, speaks of the two voyages in these terms : " The failure of the Polar expedition was *owing* to one of those *accidents* to which all sea voyages are liable, more especially when to the ordinary sea risk is superadded that of a navigation among fields and masses of ice." Now, as a mere looker on, I am inclined to think, with Phoca, that if Captain Buchan had been ordered to make *his* attempt to the *eastward* of Spitzbergen, he might perhaps have advanced further than he did ; though even if it had been possible for him to pass the Polar Axis of the Globe, he never would have reached Behring's Strait.

"Of the other Voyage (says the Reviewer) we hardly know in what terms to speak, or how to account for it." He does, however, in the sequel, seem to account for it pretty well. And, after belabouring the Captain to his heart's content with his goose-quill, he consoles *himself* under "the disappointment he experienced in common with the *rest of the world*, at the failure of the two expeditions, which *bade so fair* to set at rest the long agitated question of the existence or non-existence of a north-west passage," &c., with a glance "at the advantages which have resulted from it." The first and most prominent of them is thus candidly acknowledged ; " We are *now quite sure* that *there is* such a Bay, or rather inland sea, as that of Baffin, though neither so wide, nor of the same form, as it is usually represented in charts,"—a fact, by the by, that few or none, except himself, perhaps had ever doubted, any more than *they believed* in the existence of his imaginary current of "four or five knots velocity, through Baffin's Sea," which this recent confirmation of poor Baffin's veracity has gone far to annihilate, and with it one of the *Reviewer's strongest arguments* in favor of a practicable passage for ships ; as I shall endeavor to show by and by.

In consequence of the failure of both these expeditions, the question of a practicable passage, either by way of the Pole, or through Davis's Strait to the northward and westward, and through Behring's

Strait into the Pacific, of course remained in precisely the same doubtful state as it did before they sailed. Captain Ross had been deceived by a reliance on his own eyesight, and therefore did not examine, with all due care and attention, the entrance and extent of Lancaster Sound, which many of the Officers of the Expedition believed to be open to the westward; it was therefore thought proper to send out another expedition to explore it completely.

Many were sanguine enough to think it would be found to lead into the Polar Sea, or along the North Coast of America, whence the long sought for passage through Behring's Strait would be accomplished, and none more so than our Reviewer.

In the Quarterly Review, No. 35, at pages 211, 212, he took much pains to show that *his* " perpetual current to the southward through Baffin's Sea *did* exist, because Baffin's Bay *did not ;* as it would be difficult to explain how ANY current could originate at the bottom of such a Bay, much less a current that is stated to run sometimes with a velocity of four and even five miles an hour;" and the fact of " several vessels having been as high as Baffin, without observing the least appearance of land, removed *all doubt* as to the non-existence of the Bay, as drawn in the charts." From *his own* mind it certainly did.

In the Quarterly Review, No. 36, for June following, while the two Expeditions under Buchan and Ross were pending, he " discussed the points on which the probability of their success might be calculated ; and which he thought would mainly depend on two circumstances ; the existence of a circumvolving current from the North Pacific into the Atlantic, which would prove the communication ; and of a great Polar Sea without *land.*" As to *any obstruction from ice there,* it does not seem to have entered at all into his contemplation. He considered " the important, and indeed the *only* point to be ascertained, was the general and permanent direction taken by the great body of the Pacific."

Though he seems to have been perfectly satisfied *himself,* with " having traced the waters of the Pacific through Behring's Strait," and along with it a plank of mahogany all the way to Disco; yet the movement of those waters *towards* Behring's Strait seems to be completely disproved by Phoca's statement of facts, though he admits, on the words of Cook and Clarke, of there being a *trifling* superficial current to the northward *in* that Strait; and which has since been confirmed by Lieutenant Kotzebue. But as the Reviewer has confessed that he *does* " *now know* there *is* such a Bay, or rather inland Sea, as that of Baffin," *he* must admit the *impossibility* of the mahogany plank having drifted down to Disco, through *his* " Baffin's Sea." And yet, notwithstanding this Reviewer's acknowledgement *now,* of there being indeed such a Bay as that of Baffin, he still clings to his favorite current, as part of the circumvolving one between the Pacific and Atlantic Oceans, and will not give it up, although he formerly declared " it would be difficult to explain how *any* current *could originate* in the bottom of such a bay;" protesting in the Quarterly Review, No. 41, that " whatever Captain Ross may say or think to the contrary, there cannot remain the slightest doubt that the great body of the water in Baffin's Bay has a motion" to the southward.

This pertinacious adherence to a long cherished favorite notion, is very natural in one who had been " so circumstantial with regard to this current, as *its*

Data.   M *existence* (said he) affords, in our opinion, the *best hope* for the success of the Expeditions now engaged in exploring a passage."

Unwilling to place much confidence in the statements of the conductor of the Expedition through Davis's Strait, the Quarterly Reviewer preferred the *opinion* of the officers of the Alexander, "that a *southerly* current had been experienced, lon g before they approached the entrance of Cumberland Strait," on their return to the southward. But on this subject, in its proper order, I shall have occasion to give the opinion of the officer who *then* commanded the Alexander, and has had further experience, since that time, of the set of the currents, or tides, in Davis's Strait, as far to the northward, at least, as Lancaster Sound.

The result of Ross's Voyage having rendered a passage through "Baffin's Sea" *rather* hopeless in a *high latitude*, and the supposed current at all events very doubtful, though the Reviewer rested *his* "*best hope*" for the success of the Expedition on *its* existence ; the search was now to be made for this " best hope" further to the southward, in Sir James Lancaster's Sound.

The Hecla and Griper were commissioned for this service about the latter end of January 1819, the former by Lieutenant Edward William Parry, and the Griper by Lieutenant Matthew Liddon. They left Deptford on the 4th of May, and sailed from the Nore on the 11th. Lieutenant Parry was instructed, as Commander of the Expedition, "to make the best of his way to Davis's Strait. On his arrival in this Strait, his further proceedings were to be regulated chiefly by the position and extent of the ice ; but on finding it sufficiently open to permit his approach to the western shores of the Strait, and his advance to the northward, as far as the opening in Sir James Lancaster's Sound, he was to proceed in the first instance, to that part of the coast, and use his best endeavors to explore the bottom of that Sound ; or in the event of its proving a Strait opening to the westward, he was to use all possible means, consistently with the safety of the two ships, to pass through it, and ascertain its direction and communications ; and if it should be found to connect itself with the northern sea, he was to make the best of his way to Behring's Strait." The finding a passage from the Atlantic to the Pacific was the *main object* of this expedition. Another expedition proceeded also under the command of Lieutenant Franklin, late Commander of the Trent, from Fort York, on the shores of Hudson's Bay, to trace the Copper Mine River to its mouth, and the coast of America from thence to the eastward or northward, as the case might be, *in order to settle the long-sought-for N.E. point of that Continent.* Lieutenant Parry returned from his Voyage on the 3d of November 1820, of which he has published a well-written account. Captain Franklin returned some months before him, and both were justly promoted for the ability and perseverance with which they *endeavored* to accomplish the *grand objects* of the Expeditions they were respectively intrusted with the command of. But though they both failed in attaining the two *chief ultimate objects* of their search, owing to the existence of physical impediments which had not been foreseen, and perhaps no human power could possibly have surmounted ; yet they did as much as men could do, and brought back with them a great accession of knowledge respecting the Arctic regions, and many experimental facts, which will be found, I fear, when we come to examine them closely, to bear rather *against* than in favor of the existence of a *practicable* N.W. passage for ships, though both these officers have *recorded* their opinions of its practicability.

Though Captain Parry had the good fortune to find a navigable passage, from the entrance of Lancaster Sound, along the southern shores of a chain of lands, lying in an east and west direction, and sufficiently contiguous to keep that passage free at least of the heavy polar ices, by impeding *their* further progress between or to the southward of those lands; yet when he approached the S.W. end of the westernmost of them, named by him Melville Island, he found it utterly impossible to succeed in his most strenuous attempts to pass that point. When near this point, Captain Parry says, he sent Lieutenant Beechey to measure a mass of ice which had drifted close to the ship, who found its thickness to be 42 feet; and he says, " as it was a piece of a regular floe, this measurement may serve to give some idea of the general thickness of the ice in this neighbourhood. There were some, however, which were of much larger dimensions ; an immense floe, which formed the principal, or at least the nearest obstruction to the *westward*, was covered with large hummocks, giving to its upper surface the appearance of *hill and dale.* The thickness of this floe, at its nearest edge, was six or seven feet above the sea, and as about six sevenths are usually immersed, the whole thickness would appear, in the common way of reckoning, to have been from 40 to 50 feet, which corresponds with that actually measured by Lieutenant Beechey. But the hummocks were, many of them at least, from 15 to 25 feet above the level of the sea, so that the solidity of this enormous floe must have been infinitely greater than any thing we had seen before. It was the opinion of Messrs. Allison and Fyffe that it very much resembled the ice met with *at Spitzbergen,* but according to the account of the two latter, was much *heavier* than any which *they* had seen *there."* Captain Parry then observes—" It now became evident, from the combined experience of this and the preceding year, that there was *something peculiar* about the S.W. extremity of Melville Island, which made the *icy sea there extremely unfavorable* to navigation, and which seemed likely to bid defiance to all our efforts to proceed much further to the westward in this parallel of latitude. We had arrived off it on the 17th of September 1819, after long and heavy gales from the north-westward, by which alone the ice is ever opened on this coast" (meaning, I presume, the *south* or leeward coast *with* those winds), " and found it in unusually heavy and extensive fields, completely closing in with the land, a mile or two to the eastward of where we were now lying. We again arrived here in the early part of August; and though the rest of the navigation had been remarkably clear for the 50 miles between this and Winter Harbour, seeming to afford a presumptive proof that the season was rather a favorable one than otherwise, the same obstruction presented itself as before; nor did there appear, from our late experience, a reasonable ground to hope that any fortuitous circumstance, such as an alteration in winds or currents, was likely to remove the formidable impediments which we had to encounter. The *increased dimensions* of the ice *hereabouts* would not alone have created an insurmountable difficulty in the navigation, but that it was very *naturally* accompanied by a degree of *closeness* which seldom or never admitted an open space of clear water of sufficient size for a ship, or even a boat, to sail on it. We had been lying nearly in our present situation, with an easterly wind, and blowing fresh, for thirty-six hours together, and although this was considerably off the land, beyond the western point of the land now in sight, the ice *had not* during the whole of that time *moved a single yard from the shore ;* affording a proof that there was *no space* in which the ice was at liberty to *move to the westward.*" Captain Parry, at page 297 of his Voyage, after again admitting that " there is *something peculiar* about the S.W. end of Melville Island, extremely unfavorable to navigation, yet it is also certain, that the obstructions we met with from ice, both as to its thickness and extent, were found generally to *increase* as we proceeded to the *westward* after passing through Barrow's Strait," endeavors to account for this 'peculiar something,' as well as this increased obstruction from ice, in a way that I should rather have expected from the *Quarterly Reviewer* than him. Captain Parry says, " That we should find this to be the case, might perhaps have been reasonably anticipated ; *because* the proximity to a permanently open sea" (the Pacific I presume) " appears to be the circumstance, which of all others, tends the most to temper the severity of the Polar regions, in any given parallel of latitude. On this account, I should always expect to meet with the most serious impediment about midway between the Atlantic and Pacific Oceans ; and having once passed that barrier, I should as confidently hope to find the difficulties lessen, in proportion as we advanced towards the latter sea ; especially as it is well known that the climate of any given parallel on the west side of America is, no matter from what cause, very many degrees more temperate than on the eastern

coast." This is a very fair *theoretical* mode of account-
ing for the peculiarity of the obstructions near the
S.W. end of Melville Island, though the Quarterly
Reviewer gives a much better reason for it. He says,
" All their efforts proved of no avail to get beyond the
S.W. extremity of Melville Island. There is something
peculiar in the situation of this point that prevents the ice
from leaving the shore, as had in every other part of the
voyage been found to be the case ; it was *owing probably* to the *discontinuance* of land, *or* to the *prevailing
northerly winds having driven down* the main body of ice,
and wedged it in among the Islands." Nothing can be
more evident than that it *was* owing to *both* these
causes ; and which Mr. Fisher, the Surgeon of the
Hecla, seems very clearly to have considered so on the
spot. He says, in his Voyage of Discovery to the
Arctic regions, at page 127, on Friday 17th September, 1819, " We cast off again this morning, and stood
to the westward, until we came to the ice, which we
found to be nearly in the same situation where we
were stopped by it yesterday. It was observed to be
much heavier than what we have generally met with
before, being somewhat like that which they describe
the Greenland ice to be; so that I think it is most
probable that it is *not formed here*, but *drifts down* from
higher latitudes, or what may be termed the *Polar Sea*."
The day before this, the ship had been " made fast to a
hummock of ice aground in fifteen fathoms water,"
which must therefore have been at least 100 feet thick.
In the following year again, when in latitude 74° 26',
and longitude 113° 46', very near the S.W. extremity of
Melville Island, on the 15th of August, he says, at page
234 : " With respect to the state of the ice, I could
perceive no material difference in it to-day from what
it has been for this week past : close in with the land,

it is broken up into small pieces; but at the distance of a mile (or two at the farthest) from the coast, commence a line of floes, that extend to the westward and southward as far as the eye can penetrate from the most elevated situation in this neighbourhood, and leaving *no clear space* except a few pools." " Without digressing much from my narrative, I may remark, in this place, that the reason *generally given* why so much heavy ice should lie off this part of the coast is, *because we are* near the *west end* of this island, so that the ice which *comes from the northward* lodges here. The land (Banks's) that we see to the southward and westward (at the distance of 17 or 18 leagues) may be considered also as another locality that tends to keep this place always hampered with ice." Mr. Fisher's opinion as to the origin and cause of this heavy ice in this place, is doubtless most correct; and from what he says, it would appear to have been generally entertained on board the ships at the time. It seems indeed, from the following passage, to have been even the opinion of Captain Parry himself, that *discontinuity* of land westward of Melville Island was *one reason* why this insurmountable icy impediment, of so new a character, was found about the western extremity of that island; and which therefore necessarily involves admission of the *other primary* one, viz. the *so far* unobstructed *drift* of the ice *from the northward.* At page 250 he says, " On the 16th of August, in order to have a clear and distinct view of the state of the ice, after 24 hours' wind from that (western) quarter, Captain Sabine, Mr. Edwards, and myself, walked about two miles to the westward, along the highest part of the land, next the sea; from whence it appeared but too evident that no passage in this direction was yet to be expected. The only clear water in sight, was a channel of about three quarters of a mile wide in some places, between the ice and the land, extending as far as a bold headland bearing N. 52° W. distant two miles and a quarter, and was called Cape Dundas. The ice to the W. and W.S.W. was as solid and compact to all appearance as so much *land;* to which, indeed, the surface of many of the fields, from the kind of hill and dale I have before endeavored to describe, bore no imperfect resemblance. I have no doubt that, had it been our object to *circumnavigate* Melville Island, or, on the other hand, *had* the coast *continued its westerly direction*, instead of turning to the northward, we should have contrived to proceed a little occasionally, as opportunities offered." As to the first, it is very questionable ; but of the latter there can be no doubt at all, because, *if* the *land* had *continued* its westerly direction, no such impediment as was found, for want of its protection on the north, could have existed, as far as it might have extended. Indeed, if a chain of lands such as the North Georgian Islands extended from Melville Island all the way to the meridian of Behring's Strait, on the same parallel, the passage from thence to that Strait would be attended with no more difficulty than that was from the entrance of Lancaster Sound to Melville Island, and for exactly the same reason. But it is from the improbability (amounting almost to a certainty) that any such lands can be *reasonably* expected to exist in a direction parallel to the north coast of America, *so contiguous* to each other, *in that whole extent*, as to afford to ships the same protection from the polar ice, as the Hecla and Griper received from the North Georgian Islands, that I am compelled to infer the non-existence of a *practicable* N.W. passage for ships.

Data.   N

It being much more probable (even *admitting* that all the lands that may extend from the west side of Green-land towards the coast of America, as far even as Icy Cape, *are insulated,*) that spaces, quite as extensive as that to the westward of Melville Island, *may* intervene, so as to admit the polar ices between lands so sepa-rated, and thereby cause the very same kind of obstruc-tion as was met with at the S.W. extremity of Melville Island.

Nothing can prove more clearly than the foregoing extracts, that the ices described therein *were* what Mr. Fisher very justly considered them, *polar ices,* (if there be no land to the northward) and that such ices have, as I will endeavor to prove they must necessarily have, a constant tendency to drift to the southward, under the impulse given to them by the polar current, and the prevailing northerly winds, *until* they are impeded by the *northern* shores of intervening lands, upon which they *must* consequently lodge; as was found to be the case by Captain Parry, when he made his journey across Melville Island. He says, at page 191, "As soon as we had gained the summit of this point, which was about 80 feet above the sea, and was named after Mr. Nias, we had an additional confirmation that it was the sea which we had now reached ; the *ice being thrown* up under the point, and as far as we could see to the west-ward, in large, high, irregular masses, exactly similar to those which had so often afforded us anchorage and shelter upon the southern shores of the Island." " A continuous line of very large hummocks of ice extended from Point Nias about two miles and a half in a N.E. direction. They were the kind of hummocks which always indicate the ice having *met with resistance by grounding*. The whole of the shore, as far as I could see with a glass, bore evident marks of that *tremendous pres-sure* which is produced by fields of ice when *set in motion*." He further observes, "The ice on this coast, as compared with that in Winter Harbour, being double the thickness of that of the other, may at first sight appear to be an indication of a *more severe climate* on *this* than on the southern coast of Melville Island." Though it may appear very like presumption to question the opinion and judgment of Captain Parry, in this instance, yet I should imagine there can be no doubt of the fact of the north side of Melville Island being *colder* than the other, for the same reason that it would be *warmer* near the *south* side of a high brick-wall, than it possibly could be on the other; especially if extensive fields of ice lay to the *north* of it, and the winds prevailed nearly two-thirds of the year from that quarter, as it appears they do at Melville Island. And the *proof* of this is, that the radiation of heat from the southern shores of Melville Island dissolved the ice from those shores, but the northern continued to be encumbered with it; and in all human probability will remain so till doomsday.[1] However, Captain Parry says, "this *circumstance* is, as we know by experience, the formation of a single winter; whereas, on an *open* and *exposed beach*, like that of Point Nias, the *last year's* or sea ice is at liberty to fix itself in the autumn, forcing up the masses which we see aground in all such situations, and *increasing* in the course of the *ensuing* winter to the

---

[1] Mr. Fisher, at page 209, says, "With respect to the nature of the country on this side the island, there is as little to be said, in favor of its fertility, as any we have seen; in fact it is as barren as it is possible for land to be : even the hardy Poppy, that *abounds* on the *south side* of the island in the worst soil, is not to be seen here."

thickness which we found it to be. Had we acci-
dentally come to any bay or harbour, *secure* from the
access of the floes from without, and of the same depth
as Winter Harbour, *I doubt* not we should have found
the ice in it of nearly the same thickness." I am free to
confess that I very much doubt this inference; for
though a bay on the *north* side of the island, "secure
from the floes from without," and "of the same depth
as Winter Harbour," would be, *so far, similar;* yet the
situation of one, being to the north, open to the winds
which are found so generally to blow from that frigid
quarter, and the other on the south, having intervening
land to shelter it more from them, there would doubtless
be a difference of general temperature in favor of Winter Harbour. However, though this may be only matter of opinion, yet the *matters of fact* which the foregoing extract contains, are much more to my purpose, and
speak a language that cannot well be misunderstood. The
first of these is, that heavy masses of ice had been *forced*
up, *on* an *open* and exposed beach—open to the north.
From this first fact I infer the existence of a cause (or
causes) let it be what it may, which is in constant or
general operation of power sufficient to impel those
masses *from north* to south, and to force them by "tremendous pressure up on the beach." That the same
cause will impel these polar ices down to the southward, even on to the coast of America, wherever they
can float, and do not meet with any obstruction to their
progress; or are not dissolved. That if any of the
masses furthest to the southward be in fact dissolved,
the space they covered is imperceptibly occupied by
those next to them, which are continually pressed on
towards the south, by others still further to the northward of them. For this reason, the north shore of

Melville Island was encumbered with such polar ices, from the beach, as far out to sea, towards the north, as the sight extended at its highest elevation. And for the same reason, there can be no doubt that the *north-ern* shores of *all* lands situated between Greenland and any part of the north coast of America, must be encumbered in like manner, *unless* they be protected from the polar ices by *other* lands to the *northward of them*. Besides, ices so lodged aground may, instead of diminishing, perhaps *augment annually*, as Phoca, with proper caution and diffidence, only *inferred* as *possible*, because (what was considered) the *best authority*, at the time, informed him, " that, owing to the great depth at which ice floats in water, it must take the ground at considerable distance from the shore, where it becomes *a nucleus* for floating patches to form *round* it ; and the summer sun having little power on such enormous masses, *they accumulate* in magnitude, and spread over a *wider surface from year to year ;* and if large fragments were not frequently torn from them, and borne away by the currents, the *whole* surface of the *straits* and narrow seas would, in process of time, be covered with ice. The most *northerly* straits and islands, which form the passages into Hudson's Bay, *are of course never free* from mountains and patches of ice ; and yet all navigators proceeding on discovery have either entered those Straits and had to struggle against the ice, and currents, and tides on the coast of America; or, have kept so close to the land, on the west coast, of Greenland as to encounter the same obstacles." All this was very true, no doubt, as regarded the past, and, taken prophetically, has been proved unfortunately to be but too correct, by the result of the several attempts which have since been made to navigate these '*more northerly straits*.' Phoca was told too, " how little the influence of an Arctic summer, even, is on fields of ice, perpetually surrounded by a freezing atmosphere created by themselves ;" and this Captain Parry has furnished us with facts quite sufficient to confirm ; particularly the one observed by him on the open and exposed beach of Point Nias. *There*, he says, " the *last year's* or sea ice, is at liberty to fix itself in the autumn, *forcing* up the masses seen aground in *all* such situations, and *increasing* in the *ensuing winter*, to the thickness which we found it to be." Now here is the acknowledgement of *one* year's ice being *increased* by the *next ensuing*. Then why not an *annual* increase, till doomsday ?—*I* do not presume to say that such *can* be the result. But, on such authority, who will be bold enough to question the legitimacy of the inference, as far at least as it is applicable to ice *aground* on *northern* shores of Arctic lands ? It is true, that Phoca, before his mind was *enlightened* by the knowledge of recent facts, took it into his head that there must be some *probable cause*, counteractive of the Quarterly Reviewer's *perpetual frost ;* and explained his ideas on that subject in one of his letters. He came to the conclusion that " it was more than probable, that the process of *freezing* and *melting* might be going on in the Arctic regions, on the *same* body of floating ice (if of magnitude to be sufficiently immersed) at the *same time*, and perhaps in winter as well as in summer :" for, from a few recorded facts, he deduced the *probability* of the *progressive* general *decrease* of the temperature of the sea from the surface downwards in the *torrid* and temperate zones ; and its progressive *increase* downwards in the *frigid* zones ; both however being dependent on the atmospheric temperature at the time. He was further confirmed in this opinion by the results of two simple experiments, made in a deep wooden vessel with a tin bottom. This being filled with common pump water, a red hot plate of iron was held close to its surface, to try the first case ; and a large piece of ice was used for trial of the second case. He reserved to himself *exceptions* to these two *general* results, in the event of experiments being made on the sea's temperature, *in soundings*, and *confined waters*, near *land :* because each *general* result was found to be materially affected by putting ice to the outside of the bottom of the vessel, whilst heat was applied to the surface, in the first case ; and by putting heat at the bottom, whilst ice was applied to the surface, in the other case : and *therefore* thought it probable that the high temperature of the lands in the torrid, and perhaps the temperate zones, might in some degree be communicated to the bottom, in soundings, more especially in shoal and confined waters, and thereby cause exceptions to the general rule, similar to those in the first case ; and in the Arctic (and Antarctic) regions, under like circumstances of locality, those similar to the second case.

At page 448, in No. 36, Quarterly Review for June 1818, an extract from Davis's " World's Hydrographical Description" is given, in confirmation perhaps of an opinion expressed by the Reviewer, five or six months before, as to " the little effect of even an Arctic summer, on fields of ice perpetually surrounded by a freezing atmosphere created by themselves ;" to establish also his doctrine of " the *perpetuity* of the southern current " through " Baffin's Sea ;" and to prove that " those who have formed their notions of this current from the reveries of Saint Pierre, on the melting of the polar ice, have adopted very erroneous ideas on the subject :" for he attempts to show, on the authority of Mr. Scoresby's Meteorological Journal for 1812, to which he refers Malte-Brun, (who had dared "to convert an ice mountain into a marine current, by the effect of the *solar rays*,) that *as much* ice as the solar rays decomposed on one side of such a *mountain*, would be *re*-composed, probably, on the other." This is at least one step towards self-refutation, as it admits the *probably equal* and simultaneous operation of the two opposite powers of heat and cold *above* water, on floating ice, which would consequently keep the quantity *there equal* at all times.

But the Reviewer *now* wishes, it seems, to go further; and having since had a glimpse of some " new light," from " Mr. Scoresby's communication to Sir Joseph Banks," and the " observations made in the Greenland seas on the temperature of the water at the surface, when that of the atmosphere, he takes it for granted, (but *why*, he does not say) was at or below the freezing point," which are inserted at page 453 and 4, he thinks it as well to look a little *deeper*. And also *now*, for the first time, perhaps, looking to the fair inference that *has* been already, or might be, drawn from *his* doctrine of progressive everlasting *congelation* in the Arctic regions, he calls old Davis from the " vasty deep" to help him out with some fact to show that there *is* some *other* counteracting power in operation, *under water* also, to prevent that accumulation of ice, which " otherwise, in process of time, would freeze up the globe." Fortunately, and most opportunely, he was furnished with this by old Davis, who tells him that *he* had seen " an Ylande of Yse turne up and downe because it hath melted so faste under water." On this grand and seemingly *unexpected* discovery, the sagacious critic, in the name of his brethren, exclaims in rapture, " We have no doubt that Davis is right, and that the action of the *salt* sea on ice, and *not* its decomposition by the solar rays, prevents an accumulation which would otherwise, in process of time, freeze up the globe!!" It would seem, however, entirely to have escaped the notice of this sage critic that Davis did not account for this melting of " the yse so faste under water," because the sea was *salt*, but owing " to *his* heate of *power* to dissolve yse." The Reviewer might as well have told us *what he meant* by " the *action* of the *salt* sea on ice." It *may* have been the increased temperature of the sea, shown by the experiments of Dr. Irving and Mr. Scoresby; but if so, why apply the needless term *salt* to the sea? He was not quite *sure, then,* perhaps, of the fact of an increasing temperature of the sea downwards; as he deems " the few experiments in Phipps's Voyage wholly unsatisfactory," yet they must have made *some* impression on his belief. However, he very prudently declines hazarding " an opinion as to the *cause* of this warm stream," but leaves it to his *readers* " to ascribe it " to the " submarine geysers " of Pennant, or to " the heated current from the Pacific, which probably *loses nothing* of *its* temperature in its passage among the active Volcanoes of the Aleutian Islands," and thence through Behring's Strait, and the *Frozen Ocean*, into the bargain!! Bless us! what an advantage it is to be a man of learning and a great traveller! what daring flights it enables the mind to take on the wings of a lively imagination! The Edinburgh Reviewer, in No. 59, observes on this subject, " that, contrary to what takes place under milder skies, the water drawn up from a considerable depth is warmer within the Arctic circle than what lies on the surface. The *floating* ice accordingly begins to melt generally on the *underside,* from the slow communication of the *heat*

Data. O

sent upwards." The Quarterly Reviewer says, "but we are rather inclined to consider it as the *lighter* water *rising* from an extreme depth to the surface." Mr. Scoresby, in his account of the Arctic regions, published in 1820, says, at page 184, "As far as experiments have hitherto been made, the temperature of the sea has generally been found to diminish on descending. But *in the Greenland* sea, near Spitzbergen, the *contrary* is the *fact*. The results of the experiments he made for determining this interesting point were highly satisfactory ; the water being *invariably warmer* than that at the surface." A series of these experiments are exhibited in a table at p. 187. "They were *all* made in deep water, clear of land, and *out of soundings*, the tem, perature of the air at the times being generally below, and seldom above 32 degrees of Fahrenheit." So much for the fact, which (being an unlearned man) is all *I* dare meddle with ; but as others may wish to see whether Mr. Scoresby's attempts to account for the *cause* are more clear and satisfactory than those of the two rival Reviewers, I shall insert what he says at page 209, &c. "From the fact of the sea near Spitzbergen being usually six or seven degrees *warmer*, at the depth of 100 to 200 fathoms, than it is at the surface, it seems *not improbable* that the water *below* is a still farther extension of the *Gulf stream*, which, on meeting with water near the ice, *lighter* than itself, sinks below the surface, and becomes a counter under current." And again, " From the circumstance of an under stratum of water, in the Spitzbergen sea, being generally warmer, by some degrees, than that at the surface, though of *similar specific gravity*, it would appear that the warmer water is, in this case, the most *dense*, or why does it not rise and change places with the colder water at the surface?" I am sure *I* cannot say *why* ; and, my good reader, if you are not able to do so, perhaps one or other of the critics will assist you ; though I apprehend the Quarterly Reviewer will be somewhat puzzled by the question. For *his warm* water, brought all the way from the *Pacific* Ocean, happens to be *lighter* than that at the surface in the Arctic regions, and at an extreme depth too (as he of course can give a good reason for); but Mr. Scoresby's warm stream from the *West Indies* is *heavier* than that at the surface (or " of similar specific gravity," for it is hard to say which he means), and therefore *sinks* underneath it, instead of *rising* like the Quarterly Reviewer's circumvolving current, " from an *extreme depth* to the surface." In the Edinburgh Philosophical Journal, No. 4, for April 1820, is inserted an abstract of Mr. Scoresby's results ; also some obtained by Lieutenant Beechey, on board the Trent, in the Spitzbergen seas ; and others by Mr. Fisher on board the Dorothea.

From these and other experiments made by Dr. Marcet, the Editor of that Journal observes, " In Baffin's Bay, the Mediterranean sea, and the tropical seas, *the temperature of the sea diminishes* with the depth, according to the observations of Phipps, Ross, Parry, Sabine, Saussure, Ellis,and Peron ; but it is a remarkable fact, that in the Arctic or Greenland seas, *the temperature of the sea increases with the depth.* This singular result was first obtained by Mr. Scoresby, in a series of well-conducted experiments, and has been confirmed by the later observations of Lieutenants Franklin, Beechey, and Mr. Fisher." I however apprehend, that the correctness of the Editor's observations will sometimes, perhaps, be impeached, by results a little at variance with *both* these *general* rules, owing to the circumstances of locality as to land, *depth* of water, and the temperature of the atmosphere, compared with that of the surface, at the time of making experiments on submarine temperature. Some few instances in proof of such exceptions to the first general rule, appear by the experiments made by Captain Hall and Mr. Clarke Abel, near the coast of China, and were noticed by Phoca in his second letter ; and other exceptions to the second rule are to be found among the experiments made by recent voyagers in the Arctic regions. One is particularly noticed by Mr. Scoresby, in his " Journal of a Voyage to the Northern Whale Fishery," published last year, 1823. He says, at page 237, "At 10 A.M. being in latitude 72° 7′ and longitude 19° 11′ west, we obtained *soundings* in 118 fathoms; muddy bottom. The temperature of the sea at the surface was 34°, and within five fathoms of the bottom, by a Six's thermometer, it was 29°: the air at the same time was 42°. In all former experiments upon the temperature of the Greenland sea, I have invariably found it to be *warmer below* than at the *surface. This exception* therefore is remarkable :" and Mr. Scoresby might have added *singular* too; for it is perhaps the only experiment he ever made *in soundings,* which is quite sufficient to account for the exception. Mr. Scoresby adds: " On my first trial, made in 1810, in latitude 76° 16′, and longitude 9° east, the temperature at the depth of 1380 feet was found to be 33° 3′ (by the water brought up), whilst at the surface it was 28° 8′. In one instance (the latitude being 79° and long. 5° 40′ E.) there was an increase of 7° of temperature on descending 600 feet; and in another series of experiments, near the same place, an increase of 8° was found at the depth of 4380 feet. What renders this increase of temperature

on descending in the Spitzbergen sea the more extraordinary, is the fact, that in almost all other regions of the
globe, as far as observations have been made, a contrary
law prevails, the sea being colder below than at the
surface." But few or no experiments have been made
yet in the Antarctic sea ; and whenever they shall be, I
have very little doubt but it will be found to be the same
as it is in the Spitzbergen sea, progressively warmer in
proportion to the depth, *except* in *straits*, deep *bays*, or
inlets, and perhaps in soundings near land ; and that
the cause, whatever it may be (as Mr. Scoresby says),
which occasions the peculiar warmth in the Spitzbergen
sea, will produce the *same effect* in the *Antarctic* sea,
though *there* we cannot have recourse, either to the
circumvolving current, from the Pacific, of the Quarterly
Reviewer, or the Gulf stream of Mr. Scoresby, to assist
us to account for it. It was on the firm expectation
that this warm temperature of the Arctic seas would
be found (though it appears Mr. Scoresby had discovered it to possess this, some time before), that Phoca
presumed it might be continually dissolving ice under
water ; yet still, *on the whole*, there might, by the process
of freezing above, be an *increase* of ice in the frozen sea,
but that the *surplus* was brought out by the Polar current
round the N.E. part of Greenland ; and that consequently, " the general quantity of water in that sea remained
nearly the same at all times ; that is, taking the ice and
water together, as an aggregate quantity." Though
Capt. Parry has, as we have seen, acknowledged an
increase of ice on the *northern* shores of Melville Island,
he seems to be of opinion that the quantity of *floating*
ice is generally the *same nearly*, from what he observed
in Winter Harbour.

When there, on the 6th of July 1820, he says, at

page 217, " In all cases we found the ice to be first thawed and broken up in the shoalest water, in consequence, I suppose, of the greater facility with which the ground, at a small depth below the surface of the sea, absorbed and radiated the sun's rays; and as it is in such situations that water generally freezes first, this circumstance seems a remarkable instance of the provision of nature for maintaining such a balance in the quantity of ice *annually formed* and *dissolved,* as shall prevent any undue or extraordinary accumulation of it in *any part* of the Polar regions of the earth. Among the means also which nature employs in these regions to *dissolve*, during the *short summer*, the ice which has been formed upon *the sea* by the cold of *winter*, there appears to be none more efficacious than the numerous streams of water produced by the melting of the snow upon the land, which, for a period of at least *six or seven weeks*, even in the climate of Melville Island, are continually discharging themselves into the ocean. On this account it would appear probable that the high land is more favorable to the dissolution and dispersion of ice near its shores, than that which is *lower*, because it supplies a never-ceasing flow during the whole of the thawing season." Considering the quantity of land, already known to exist between the west side of Greenland and the coast of America, and generally described *high*, this abundant dissolution therefrom must, during that period, increase the quantity of fluid, and consequently occasion *some* current towards the south. I merely mention this now, as I shall perhaps in the course of this inquiry be able to bring forward the testimony of Captain Parry to prove the fact; but *not* that the " short summer" dissolves *all* " the ice formed on the sea in winter."

We have already seen that the grounds originally taken by the Quarterly Reviewer in favor of the existence and practicability of a N.W. passage (of both which he did not then, still less does he now, entertain any doubt) are the following, which I shall again call to the reader's attention.

1st. The existence of a perpetual current setting down from the northward, from the Polar Basin, through Baffin's Sea, and Davis's Strait, into the Atlantic, with a velocity of four, and sometimes of five miles an hour.

2d. The non-existence of Baffin's Bay, as drawn in the charts.

3d. A circumvolving current, setting as perpetually " from the Pacific through Behring's Strait" *into* the Polar Basin, and *out of it* into the Atlantic ; and " whose *existence* in his opinion affords the best hope for the success of the expeditions engaged in exploring a passage into the Pacific"—by way of the Pole, as well as along the north coast of America.

4th. A great Polar sea, *free from ice*, near the Pole, *if* free from *land*.

Mr. Barrow, one of the secretaries at the Admiralty, appears, from what he says in his account of the voyages to the Polar regions, published in 1818, to have taken up the question precisely on the *same grounds* as the Reviewer.

Mr. Scoresby, in his account of the Arctic regions, published in 1820, enumerates some of these, and also considers them as probable grounds for supposing that such a passage *may exist.* Ellis's reasons, he says, appear to him to be "the most satisfactory." One of these, rather a curious one to be so " satisfactory," is " the direct testimony of the Indians, which tends to *prove* that they have seen the sea beyond the mountains, and *observed vessels navigating thereon ! !*" Where, in the name of Heaven, could these vessels have come from? or how could any have been *there*, unless they were the *canoes* of Esquimaux? which it may be presumed Ellis did not understand these Indians to mean by what he termed vessels.

Mr. Scoresby, on the whole, however, is rather sceptical on the *practicability* of such passage, "and even if it were discovered, he conceives it would be at intervals only of years that it would in all probability be open at all." Like a man of much experience and judgment, he says, " the most certain (and I dare say he might have *added* the *only*) method of ascertaining the existence of a communication between the Atlantic and the Pacific, along the northern shore of America, would doubtless be by journeys on land." This hint has been taken, and as far as it goes, successfully acted on. If followed up as it is now reported it *will be*, this " grand question," I have not the slightest doubt, *will be solved:* but by any ship or ships, *without* the aid of expeditions by land—it will remain as it now is, a matter of doubt.

Let us now examine the four grounds of argument in favor of the practicability of a N.W. passage for ships.

Phoca attempted, in the first instance, before the expeditions sailed, to disprove them all, (and I think with some success) except the 4th, which he thought probable, but desired further proof, which is still wanting.

Mr. Scoresby disputed none but the 4th, and his reasons for not believing that there is an open sea clear of ice about the Pole, I shall examine in the proper place. But let us first try the validity of all these four grounds or arguments, by the test of the experience of those navigators, who have recently visited the north Polar regions.

1st. "The existence of a perpetual current, setting down from the northward, from the Polar Basin, through Baffin's Sea, and Davis's Strait, into the Atlantic, with a velocity of four, and sometimes five miles an hour."

Although the already noticed candid declaration of the Reviewer, that ' he *now knows* there *is* such a bay as that of Baffin,' &c. and he said, before he believed it, that *if* there were such a bay, ' it would be difficult to explain how *any current could* originate at the bottom of it,' would seem to render it superfluous to *prove* that there is *no such* current, yet though I shall produce the testimony to that effect, of one whom he has had no reason to doubt, I must state the currents as I find them mentioned in Captain Ross's Voyage, from the day he passed the parallel of Cape Farewell, during his passage up to the head of Baffin's Bay, and down it again till he got off the entrance of Cumberland Strait.

On 23d of May, in lat. 57° 2′ and longitude 43° 2′, Captain Ross says : ' This evening I remarked the appearance of a current, and the next day ascertained by hoisting out our boat, that it set *W.N.W.* (true) at the rate of a quarter of a mile an hour.' On the 24th ' the *N.W.* current was still manifest.' On the 26th of May, in latitude 58° 36′, and long. 51° W. ' The latitude agreed, but we had been set by a current a few miles to the *westward.*' On the 27th, ' a copper cylinder with a detail of our situation was thrown overboard near a very large iceberg, in lat. 61° N. and long. 53° 25′, which we passed at 9 P.M. It apparently drifted to the *westward,* though we could perceive *no current.*' June 1st, in lat. 63° 41′, long. 55° 42′, ' *no effect* of a current was apparent, and having gained three miles

Data.   P

of latitude, it seemed evident there could *be no current :* which appeared surprising, as the wind had blown for three successive days directly down the strait,' that is, from the northward. On the 5th of June, lat. 65° 46', and long. 55° W. 'a boat was anchored to try for a current, but none was perceptible.' July 3d, in lat. 71° 33' and long. 56° 2', 'by mid-day we had made a degree of latitude through a channel apparently *void* of *any current.*' July 19th, 'we continued in the midst of the ice, which was *carrying* us *fast* to the *northward.*' August 13th, lat. 75° 54', long. 65° 53', 'it is worthy of remark, that here, as on the whole of this coast north-ward of 70°, we found the deepest water near the land, and that *no current* was found.'

August 23d, 'the sun's meridional altitude was ob-served on the iceberg, and the latitude found to be 76° 37', the iceberg having drifted three miles to the *north-ward.*' September 1st, lat. 73° 37', long. 77° 25', 'to observe the current, the line was dropped over again, and the transit bearings of two objects on the land set; these however did not vary in the least, nor did we find *any current* by the line.' 'My orders to stand well to the north' had been already fully obeyed, and *no current* had been found ; and if 'a current of some force' did exist, as from 'the best authorities' we had reason to believe was the fact, it could be no where but to the *southward of this latitude.*'

On the 6th of September, in lat. 72° 23', and long. 73° 7', '*no current* was found.' September 30, lat. 64° 10', and longitude 63° 5', 'we found by our reckoning that the current had set us twenty-five miles *to the N.E.* during the last 24 hours.' Thus, according to Captain Ross, *no current from the northward* was ever experienced ; but, on the contrary, when *any* could be detected, it set either *to the West, N.W., North,* or *N.E.*

Let us now see what Captain Parry discovered in his subsequent voyage, as far to the northward as the entrance of Lancaster Sound.

On the 26th of June 1819, 'in lat. 63° 59' and longitude 61° 48', in 125 fathoms, the deep sea line indicated *a drift* to the S. by W.' July 11th, ' we sounded at noon in 202 fathoms, lat. 69° 24' and longitude 58° 16'; not allowing current, which for the three preceding days had *appeared* to set the ships *to the S.S.E.* at from 8 to 13 miles per day.' July 20th, lat. 72° 57', long. 58° 41', in 120 fathoms, the ships drift *to S.S.W.*' July 24th, lat. 72° 59' and longitude 60° 8', 'ships drift to S. 1° E. 4⅔ *miles* in 24 *hours*, depth of water 260 fathoms.'

On the 30th July, noon, latitude 74° 1', 'being the first meridional altitude taken for four days, and differing only *two miles* from the dead reckoning ;' which is remarkable, considering the sluggishness of the compasses ; and would seem to afford a *presumptive proof* that ' *no southerly* current exists in *this* part of Baffin's Bay.' Further to the southward, however, in the narrowest part of Davis's Strait, he appears from the foregoing extracts to have met with a very small set of current from the northward. We will now refer to his observations when returning from Lancaster Sound, homeward bound.

On the 3d of September, in latitude 71° 24', ' being only 2 miles and ¾ to the southward of the dead reckoning in *three days*, we considered that there could be *no current of any importance* setting in that direction on this part of the coast.' September 4th, ' the latitude observed was 71° 2' 42", agreeing to within a mile of the account ; so that *no current* could well have existed since the preceding day's observation.' September 9th, in latitude 69° 24', long. 67° 5', in 35 fathoms, 5 or 6 miles from the land,

Captain Parry says, ' found the *current* running somewhat less than a mile an hour, in a *S.½E.* direction. At
4 30′ P.M. it was again tried, and found to set to the
S.E. at the rate of ¾ of a mile per hour ; and at 7 o'clock,
when we hove to near Cape Kater for the Griper to join
us, we found it to be slack water ;' which proves this to
have been a *tide stream*, and not a current. On the 11th
of September, at noon, in lat. 69° 19′, and long. 66° 5′,
in 275 fathoms : ' It must here be remarked, that for
each of the last three days, and *for these only*, we had
found the ship between 7 and 8 miles to the *southward*
of the reckoning.' September 25th, at noon, in latitude
66° 13′, ' being 2 *miles* and ¾ to the southward of the dead
reckoning, *which difference* had occurred on each of the
12 preceding days.' From all these facts it is quite
clear that no *such* current as the Quarterly Reviewer
imagined, was found—indeed scarcely any worth mention ; and certainly, what *little* was detected either in
Baffin's Bay, or Davis's Strait, could hardly have originated in *his* circumvolving current from the Pacific
through Behring's Strait and the Polar Sea : nay, there
was no such thing as a permanent current *from the westward* found in any part, even of Lancaster Sound, and
Barrow's Strait, if the authority of Captain Parry is sufficient to show it. He sums up the matter in these
words : " Of the current which we experienced in
Davis's Strait, and Baffin's Bay. It would appear that
during the *Summer* and *Autumn*, there is in this part a
considerable set to the southward. In judging of the
causes which produce this general tendency of the *superficial* current, it will be proper to bear in mind two facts,
which we have had occasion to remark in the course of
this and the preceding voyage ; first, that in a sea
much encumbered with ice, a current is almost invaria-

bly produced, immediately on the springing up of every breeze of wind ; and, secondly, that in several instances where the ships have been beset in the ice, the *direction* of the daily drift has been the point of the compass directly *opposite to that of the wind, whether* the latter was from the *northward* or the *southward*.

" It appears to me, *upon the whole*, that the southerly current which we have been enabled to detect, is *not more* than may be *caused* by the *balance* of the *northerly winds, added* to the *annual dissolution* of large quantities of snow, which finds the readiest outlet into the Atlantic. In the Polar sea, to the westward of Barrow's Strait, *no current* has been found to exist beyond *that* which is *evidently occasioned* by *different winds*. In every part which we had an opportunity of visiting, the tides, though *small*, appear to be as regular as in any part of the world." Thus the Reviewer's first ground has been annihilated by proof positive. The second he has himself confessed to be so, by the *same* proof. With respect to the third, " a circumvolving current setting as perpetually from the Pacific through Behring's Strait *into* the Polar basin, and *out* of it into the Atlantic," &c. the foregoing facts show that *none* of it was found in the whole space between the west coast of ,Greenland and the meridian of 113° 46′ 43″ 5 in lat. 74° 46′ 25″, which was the farthest point Captain Parry reached ; when the Reviewer says, " After struggling till the 16th, Captain Parry determined to return to the eastward along the edge of the ice, with the intention of availing himself of any opening that might occur, to get to the southward, and, if possible, upon the coast of America." Not perhaps, for the purpose of "*seeking*," like Captain Ross, as the Reviewer tells him, " for *his* circumvolving current ;" but for, what *Captain Parry considered* a much *better reason*, which I shall have occasion to mention by-and-by, as he assigned it at the time, and on a subsequent occasion; especially as the Reviewer has repeated it in terms of approval and acquiescence. He may also have an eye to the discovery of this favorite current of his; for as it had not been found, either by Ross or Parry, any where within the limits I have before mentioned, its progress from Behring's Strait (*if it exist beyond it*) through channels of communication, between the "Polar basin" and the Atlantic must, of course, be sought for hereafter, on parallels *between* Melville Island and the coast of America: for we cannot be surprised at the Reviewer's anxiety to get hold of a current, "whose" very "existence in his opinion affords the *best hope* for the success of the expeditions engaged in exploring a passage into the Pacific." That there certainly is a *temporary* and "*trifling*" superficial current *in* Behring's Strait to the northward, Phoca has admitted; and so do I, though totally inadequate to supply that which is known to set to the southward, continually, out of the Polar sea, through the Spitzbergen sea, into the Atlantic; even if it were possible to believe that the waters of the Pacific composed any part of it. Mr. Scoresby appears (as I before observed) to believe in the existence of the Reviewer's circumvolving current, or at least that of "a sea communication" between the Pacific and "the Atlantic." As to the latter, for water and fish, I admit it *may* be very possible, somewhere in the space between Melville Island and the north coast of America, which yet remains to be explored. Mr. Scoresby is of the same opinion as the Reviewer, chiefly for the *same* reasons; one of which is, because "it is presumed that worm-eaten driftwood, found in the Arctic countries, is derived from a trans-polar region," as he supposes one log was which "he observed in 1817, on the Island of Jan Mayen." Now, at page 209 of his "Account of the Arctic Regions," Mr. Scoresby has informed us, that "From the coast of Britain, the northern branch of the Gulf-stream *probably* extends superficially along the shore of Norway. About the North Cape, its direction appears to be changed by the influence of a westerly current from Nova Zembla, so that it afterwards sets to the *N. W.* as high as the borders of the ice, and thus operating against the *polar current* setting to the *southward.*" I should like to know Mr. Scoresby's authority for this movement of the superficial waters *towards* the *W.* and N.W. *from Nova Zembla.* However, as he of course believes, or knows it to be so, I would ask him if, by the aid of *such* a medium, the worm-eaten drift-wood he saw on Jan Mayen's Island might not have been brought from the West Indies, by this much *shorter*, and more *probable* route than the other? The polar current, Mr. Scoresby (page 4,) informs us, "flows, he is well assurèd, during nine months of the year, if not all the year round, from the N.E., towards the S.W. The velocity of this current may be from 4 to 20 miles a day, varying in different situations, but is most considerable near the coast of Old Greenland." Here, then, is the perfectly well authenticated fact of a perpetual current out of the Polar sea. It is acknowledged by the Reviewer in various parts of his writings, and particularly pointed out by Mr. Barrow, at page 377 of his Voyages to the "Polar Regions."—Now, this perpetual current to the southward, out of the Polar Sea, must have a *cause.* *That* cause, whether it be what Phoca attempted to prove it to be, or *any other*, would, doubt-less, produce a similar current from the Polar sea to-

wards the Atlantic, through *any* channels of communication which *may exist* from the west side of Greenland
to the coast of America, in quantity and velocity propor-
tionate to the dimensions of such channels.—Phoca,
disbelieving the existence of any such current in the
space called "Baffin's Sea," by the Reviewer, rationally
concluded that therefore there must be either land or
shoals *north* of that space.

The subsequent proof of Baffin's veracity, and consequently there being in fact *no such* current, either
there, or in the space westward, as far as Melville
Island, proves, that there *can be no channels* of communication *in that space* between the Polar Sea and the
Atlantic, even for *water* in any considerable quantity ;
much less for *ships*. The Reviewer, however, is of a very
different opinion. He thinks there may be a pàssage to
the northward into the Polar sea through *Wellington
Channel ;* because, when the ships passed its southern
entrance, it was "free from every particle of ice, as far
as the eye could reach, on a remarkably clear day ;"
and therefore, if the ships had proceeded up that channel, wherever it led to, the sea beyond would also have
been as clear and open. I admit it to be very possible,
that the northern opening of such channel may be
found clear of ice, as well as the southern ; *provided other
lands* lie to the *northward of it.* For one of my arguments is, that the *northern* shores of *all Arctic lands,* as
well as the northern entrances of all channels formed
between them, *if no land exist north of them, are,* and
of necessity *must be,* continually more or less encumbered with heavy polar ices ; extending from those
lands towards the north polar axis of the globe. And
that too, whether around *it* as a centre, there may be
some expanse of *open sea,* as the Reviewer, and many

others suppose, *without ice,* or whether there be, as Mr. Scoresby concludes, (page 311,) " A continent of ice-mountains, existing in regions near the Pole, yet unexplored, the nucleus of which may be as ancient as the earth itself, and its *increase* derived from the sea and atmosphere combined"—for it is quite immaterial to my argument which theory may be correct. The only facts I require are, first, the existence of heavy polar ices ; and, secondly, the certain *general movement* of these ices, *from the north* towards the south, in all the regions surrounding the Pole, as long as they are at liberty to do so, by the combined influence of the polar current, and winds prevailing from the same quarter. These facts, it is quite notorious, all parties *are agreed in ;* and have been acknowledged, over and over again, by the Reviewer, Mr. Scoresby, Mr. Barrow in his Voyages into the Polar Regions, Mr. Fisher, and Capt. Parry, in their respective publications. The Quarterly Reviewer, in his notice of Capt. Parry's Voyage, seemed to be more than ever confirmed in his opinion of an open Polar Sea by that of Dr. Brewster, who, " after comparing the results of the expedition under Capt. Parry with those he had drawn from a previous theory," is of opinion " that the hopes which have been so reasonably entertained of reaching the Pole itself, are thereby encouraged ;" concluding that " the mean temperature of the Pole of the globe will be 11°, incomparably warmer than the regions in which Capt. Parry spent the winter." The Doctor adds, "*if* the Pole is (be) placed in an open sea, the difficulty of reaching it *entirely ceases.*"

Thus supported in his opinion of a clear, open, and navigable Polar Sea, by that of "all the Greenlandmen," (*except* Mr. Scoresby), and the *theory* of the

Data.   Q

learned Doctor into the bargain, and having assured us, that he considered "the knowledge acquired on the late expedition to have afforded a sanguine hope for the complete solution of the interesting question of a north-west passage," I must confess I expected he had perhaps recommended the higher powers to make another attempt by way of the *Pole:* especially as all the original motives for sending Captain Buchan that way, must have been evidently *strengthened* in *his* mind, by the recently acquired knowledge. Nothing in fact having happened that could possibly tend to weaken them, except Capt. Buchan's failure, owing "to one of those *accidents* to which all sea voyages are liable;" unless indeed Mr. Scoresby's book may have acted as a sort of damper to the "sanguine hope" in that quarter, if ever the Reviewer has condescended to read such passages as these.

At page 49 of Scoresby's account of the Arctic Regions, he says, "Were the mean temperature of the Pole, indeed, above the freezing point of sea water, and the mean heat of latitude 78° as high as 33° or 34°, then the circumpolar seas would have a chance of being free from ice: but while the temperature of the former can be shown to be about 18°, and the latter 11° below the freezing temperature of the sea, we can have no reasonable ground, I conceive, for doubting the continual presence of ice in all the regions immediately surrounding the Pole." And at page 54: "If the masses of ice which usually prevent the advance of navigators beyond the 82nd degree of north latitude be extended in a contiuued series to the Pole (of which, *unless* there *be land* in the way, I have no doubt), the expectation of reaching the Pole by sea must be altogether *chimerical*." Now, if we take Mr. Scoresby to be right in his conjecture that "there *is* a continent of ice-mountains in the regions near the Pole, *unless* there *be land* in the way," what must there be between it and the place where Capt. Parry wintered at, which, according to Dr. Brewster's theory, is 11° or 12° colder than the Pole, or, as the Reviewer says we may conclude, " one of the *coldest spots* on the face of the globe ?" According to Mr. Scoresby, in this case there must be a frozen Ocean, north of lands surrounding that Ocean, *if* there be *no* other land between them and the pole ; which is very far *beyond* what Phoca has ventured to suppose the ice extended. On the other hand, our oracle the Reviewer says, " If we suppose that clusters of *Islands* continue to be scattered over it (the Polar Sea) on all sides, to the very Pole, or its vicinity, we shall in *that case* probably not be far from the fact, in concluding the whole of this extensive sea to be shallow, *choked up with* ice, and unnavigable." According to *this* authority, then, this Polar Sea is to be choked up with ice, *if there be land.* So that, take either view, or combine both, we can come at nothing but ice, ice, ice, all along the northern shores of Arctic lands, and a frozen ocean to some indefinite extent to the northward of the *northernmost* of those lands. Being obliged, at this rate, to give up the idea of any further attempts being intended by way of the *Pole*, as perhaps the Reviewer himself had done long before, I next considered what other particular knowledge had been acquired on the late expedition, to afford this " sanguine hope," and whereabouts the Reviewer could reasonably expect it to be realized. I could hardly suppose he would recommend another trial to be made to the northward in Baffin's Bay ; "because it is now *known* that there *is* such a bay." Nor by the route last pursued

by Capt. Parry, although, *so far*, successfully ; because
" he did not think that the strenuous, but unsuccessful
endeavors of the late expedition, in two different seasons, to penetrate to the westward of Melville Island,
afforded *any hope* that the passage will *ever* be effected
in *that* particular parallel of latitude : nor by the Wellington Channel " in the first instance," though he says
" it *may* be desirable to look at the state of the Polar
sea beyond it, *hereafter*." But, above all others, it
never could be supposed that *he* would recommend the
attempt to be made by way of Hudson's Strait and
Bay, who had reprobated the very idea from the first.
Nay, he had recorded his decided opinion that " all
former attempts had failed, because not one of them was
ever made near that part of the coast of America, round
which, it is most likely the passage would lead into the
northern or frozen ocean," a *frozen* ocean (by the by),
which he *then* believed to be *without ice.* And because
"hitherto most of our adventurers have worked their way
through Hudson's Strait, which is generally choked up
with ice ; then, standing to the northward, have had to
contend with ice *drifting to the southward*, with contrary
winds and currents ;" and " the most northerly straits
and islands, which form the passages into Hudson's
Bay, are of course never free from mountains and
patches of ice ; and yet all navigators proceeding on
discovery have either entered these Straits and had
to struggle against the ice and currents, and tides on
the coast of America, or, &c."

If we may judge from the late second fruitless attempt of Capt. Parry, to discover a passage *that way*,
the Reviewer's early judgment, in this particular instance, has unfortunately been but too correct.

For although Captain Parry did not, as far as the

newspapers tell us, meet with any greater difficulties
than the annual ships of the North-West Company generally do, in Hudson's Strait ; yet, after entering Hudson's Bay, he, like most of our adventurers, had to contend, not merely " with ice drifting to the southward,"
but was obstructed in his advance towards the N.W.
by the Repulse Bay of Middleton, whose testimony to
its existence, it appears, was doubted by himself as well
as the reviewer, who says, Middleton " looked into what
he was pleased to call Repulse Bay :" a name, however,
which has now become doubly appropriate, as well as
the Bay of Baffin. It may be allowed us to presume,
that the Quarterly Reviewer, who recorded his decided
judgment against making any future attempt, where
all former ones had failed, could not have been *consulted*
before it was resolved to send Captain Parry by *that
very route*. For as nothing had been done, or become
known, between the years 1817 and 1821, to alter the
grounds of his judgment in that particular, *he* could
not, it may be supposed, have been so inconsistent as to
have approved in the latter year, what he so decidedly
condemned in the former. He may, however, have been
persuaded to concur in the opinion of others, contrary
to what appears to have been his own better judgment
in this particular instance. Indeed the writer of the
critique on Captain Parry's first Voyage, in the 49th
No. of the Quarterly Review, says, (whilst the last expedition was pending,) Captain Parry " has recorded
his opinion in favour of its accomplishment, and *his suggestion* has *no doubt* been adopted on the present voyage :" and " it can scarcely be doubted then, that the
attempt is now about to be made, as *recommended by
Captain Parry*, in a more southern latitude, and close
along the north coast of America, where they may rea-

sonably hope to meet with a better summer climate, and a longer season for their operations, by at least six weeks."

Here then we find that the 'sanguine hope' was fully expected to be realized *on the north coast of America*, if Captain Parry had been fortunate enough to reach it by way of Hudson's Bay, and any of its northern straits. But he found those he examined blocked up with ice, which the Reviewer told us long ago they were 'never free from.' I have not heard whether any of the Reviewer's '*mountains* of ice' were met with there. However, we shall hear when Captain Parry's account of his last voyage comes out, which I am very anxious to see, in the hope of getting some more *light* thrown on the subject ; though I must confess that hope is not *very sanguine* as far as regards what may, or may not, be hereafter effected along the north coast of America. In the mean time, whilst the next expedition is pending, which I am told is to proceed by way of Lancaster Sound and down Prince Regent's Inlet, towards that coast, let us try the strength and solidity of the reasons given by the Reviewer, in his critique on Captain Parry's voyage, as well as those published by Captain Parry himself. The Reviewer in many passages has nearly quoted that officer's words, and as some of his opinions are the same, (though others very different,) they may be considered as jointly belonging to both : the one by original suggestion, and the other by adoption. I shall quote from both, and occasionally compare them together, drawing such conclusions from the *data they furnish*, as shall appear to me to be fair and legitimate ; and wherever these are at all at variance with, or tend to undermine, their own arguments, such discordance shall be pointed out.

In the first place, Captain Parry says, at page 142, " I began to consider whether it would not be advisable, whenever the ice would allow us to move, to sacrifice a few miles of the westing we had already made, and run along the margin of the floes, in order to endeavour to find an opening leading to the southward ; by taking advantage of which we might be enabled to prosecute the voyage to the westward in a lower latitude. I was the more inclined to make this attempt from its having long become evident to us, that the navigation of this part of the Polar Sea is only to be performed by watching the occasional openings between the ice and the shore : and that therefore a *continuity of land* is essential, if not *absolutely necessary* for the purpose. *Such* a continuity of land, which was *here* about to fail us, *must necessarily* be furnished *by the northern coast of America*, in whatever latitude it may be found." Again, at page 297, Captain Parry says, " Our experience, I think, has clearly shown that the navigation of the Polar Seas can never be performed with any degree of certainty without a *continuity of land.* It was only by watching the occasional openings between the ice and the shore that our late progress to the westward was effected, and *had the land continued* in the *desired direction,* there can be no question that we should have continued to advance, however slowly, towards the completion of our enterprise." " In this respect therefore, as well as in the improvement to be expected in the climate, there would be a *manifest advantage* in making the attempt *on the coast of America,* where we are sure that *land will not fail us."* In both these extracts it is declared that a continuity of land is *essential,* if not *absolutely necessary.* A continuity, where? and how situated, as to the *westward course* to be steered by ships ? Why a continuity, such as the North Georgian

Islands, lying contiguous to each other, nearly east and west, on a parallel, *north*, or on the starboard hand of that course. But why should it lie in that direction, and be situated *north of that course?* Because *such* a continuity did in fact enable the ships to proceed *as far only* to the westward as it extended, but no farther. How did it enable them to do so? By protecting them from polar ices, such as were met with at the west end of Melville Island; where, Captain Parry says, " *had* the *land continued* in the *desired direction,* there can be no question that we should have continued to advance towards the completion of our enterprise." The Quarterly Reviewer says, " the heavy ice found there was owing probably to the *discontinuance of land,* or to the *prevailing northerly winds* having *driven* down the main body of ice and *wedged* it in among the Islands." This was a *discontinuance of land on the north* of the ship's course ; and the acknowledgment of the ice " having been driven down" implies the belief that there must be a fertile supply from that quarter, and what Captain Parry terms a power in constant operation of " enormous pressure" to have thus " wedged it *in* among the Islands." Mr. Fisher, whom I have quoted before, seems to have had a much clearer conception of this matter, at the time and place, than any of his shipmates. His words are decidedly to the point, at page 99 : " I think it is probable, as long as we find *land to the northward, to stop the polar ice* from *drifting down upon us,* that we shall find a passage to the westward along the land. I do not mean, however, to say that a passage will, without any interruption, be constantly found to exist between the land and the ice : on the contrary, I am aware that a southerly wind may give us occasional checks, by forcing the ice in with the coast; but immediately the wind changes to the opposite direction, it will necessarily have the contrary effect. This is not indeed a matter of speculation, nor do I intend it to be considered as such ; for both this and the last year's experience have afforded us so many instances of the truth of what I have said, that I have no hesitation in giving it as my opinion, that the vicinity of *land to the northward* will always be in our *favor.* My object in being so particular on this point is, because there are some amongst us of quite a *different opinion.*" Mr. Fisher does not particularly name any who thus differed from him in this opinion, which he had so justly formed ; but it would appear that Captain Parry himself, before he reached Wellington Channel, regarded this " continuity of land to *the northward*" of him, with " uneasiness, principally from the possibility that it might take a turn to the southward and unite with the coast of America ;" not being then aware, as he afterwards learnt by experience that *such* continuity was " essential, if not *absolutely necessary,* for the navigation of this part of the Polar Sea ;" and as I dare say it will be for the navigation of that part of it, from the meridian of Prince Regent's Inlet to that of Icy Cape.

We have seen already *where* and *what* this continuity was, as well as its importance to the ships, as far as it extended. That importance was fully proved by the insurmountable icy obstruction which they met with at its western extremity. And yet Captain Parry says, and the Reviewer repeats it : " *Such* continuity of land as was *here* about to fail us, *must necessarily* be furnished by the *northern* coast of America, in whatever latitude it may be found."

" There would be a *manifest advantage* in making the attempt on the coast of America, where we are sure

Data.   R

that land will *not fail us.*" If the *Reviewer* alone had
made such an observation as the first, it need not have
surprised one ; but that Captain Parry himself, with the
facts of his experience before him, should not only have
written but published the same, is indeed somewhat
unexpected ; for the two cases cannot possibly have
any feature *alike*, except as regards the term continuity
applied to them, and perhaps being so, in both having
a direction nearly east and west. Though there must
be continuity of land on the coast of America, yet surely
it cannot be *such* a continuity as that formed by the
North Georgian Islands, which failed Captain Parry at
the west end of Melville Island : because the coast of
America is on the larboard hand, or to the *southward* of
ships steering to the *westward*, and consequently to
leeward, as the *prevailing* winds are from the *northward*.
On the contrary, the continuity formed by the North
Georgian Islands is to the *northward*, or on the *starboard* hand, of ships so steering, and therefore to *windward*. As to *situation*, then, they are only as opposite
as north and south. But in other and far more important points they are quite the reverse of each other.
The chain of lands extending from Baffin's Bay,
on the north of the passage discovered by Captain
Parry, acted as a barrier against the polar ices, which,
it is confessed by all the authorities I quote, are driven
from north to south by the combined power of the polar
current and "the prevailing northerly winds." The
southern shores of those lands being *weather* shores,
(or having the wind blowing *from them*,) were consequently found to be *comparatively* free from ice. Nor
in truth was there, in the whole extent of that passage,
any such heavy polar ice met with, as was found near
the west end of Melville Island. But what was the state
of the *northern* coast of Melville Island, which was a *lee*

shore, as the winds are proved to prevail? Captain Parry has told us what he observed at Point Nias. Nay, what was the state of the shores *facing the north* of the lands forming the south side of that passage, and extending from Prince Regent's Inlet to Banks's land, at whatever distance those lands may be from the North Georgian Islands? Those lands were not seen all the way in continuity, but there must be land there sufficiently contiguous to prevent the field ice even from moving further to the southward than it was observed to do from the North Georgian Islands; and *if* there should be no land nearer to those Islands than the coast of America itself, *that coast* must be the impediment, and the ice will be, in all human probability, found to be continuous quite to that coast. Now, let us see what answer Captain Parry will furnish to the last question, as to the state of the ice to the southward.

It has already been seen, at page 142 of Captain Parry's Voyage, that, when he first met with such decided obstruction, near the west end of Melville Island, he "was desirous of finding an opening in the ice leading to the *southward*, by taking advantage of which, he might be enabled to prosecute the voyage to the *westward* in a *lower latitude*." At page 250, he describes the ice to the W. and *W.S.W.* of Cape Dundas, from whence, it being 1000 feet high, the view of it must have been very extended. " It was as solid and compact as so much land ; no passage in that direction was yet to be expected ; the only clear-water in sight was a channel of about three-quarters of a mile wide, between the ice and the land."—At page 259, on the 26th of August, when he cast off from the ice, and made all sail to the eastward, he says, " We kept close along the edge of the ice, which was *quite compact to the southward, without the smallest appearance of an open-* *ing* to encourage *a hope* of penetrating in *that direction."* At page 261, when in lat. 72° 2′ 15″ and long. 105° 14′ 20″, he says, " A constant look-out was kept from the crow's-nest, for an *opening to the southward;* but not a *single break* could be *perceived* in the mass of ice which still *covered the sea in that direction."* And on the following day, the 28th of August, he adds, " The ice to the *southward,* along which we continued to sail this day, was composed of floes, remarkable for their extraordinary length and continuity : some of them not having a single break or crack for miles together, though their height above the sea was generally not more than 12 inches, and their surface as smooth and even as a bowling-green ; forming a *striking contrast* to the ice to which we had lately been accustomed more westerly." On the 30th of August, he says, " Having now traced the ice the whole way, from long. 114° to 90° *without discovering any opening* to encourage a hope of penetrating to *the southward,* I could not entertain the slightest doubt that there no longer remained a possibility of effecting our object." Does Captain Parry then, with facts like these before his eyes, really mean to say, that a continuity of land, *south* of the *westerly* course to be steered towards Behring's Strait, *is* in any point, except the two I have mentioned, *such* as one to the *north* of it? Suppose, for instance, that, after he entered Lancaster Sound, there had been *no land* whatever to the *northward,* between him and the Pole, and that the land to the southward from Cape Byam Martin to Banks's Land, or even to Behring's Strait, was continuous; I would ask him candidly, to say, if he believes he *could* have advanced to the westward beyond even the 80th degree of longitude?

Would he have found *that* continuity *such* as the one to the *northward*, whose existence *alone* enabled him to reach the 114th meridian? But the Quarterly Review would perhaps answer for him : " Yes, he would not only have made as much westing as he did, but he would have reached Behring's Strait ; because he would have entered *my* ' *Polar basin*,' where there would have been *no ice* to impede his progress." And yet the Reviewer acknowledges that " the *ice* found about the S.W. extremity of Melville Island, was owing probably to the *discontinuance* of land, or to the prevailing northerly winds having *driven down* the main body, and *wedged* it in among the Islands !" May I ask him then to give me any sound reason, *why* the same combined causes should *not* have produced the same effects, *if* that discontinuance had taken place in the same parallel on *any other* meridian, between Baffin's Bay and 114° *west* longitude? and why it may not take place at the west end of Arctic lands, on *any meridians west* of that longitude, and in parallels even *south of Melville Island*, IF NO OTHER LANDS should happen to be situated to the NORTHWARD of them again? He, however, I dare say, will not allow the inference that must be drawn from his own admission : for in the face of that admission, and in support of his firm belief still, that there is an open Polar Sea, notwithstanding ice " is *driven* to the southward" from thence, where the supply *must* consequently come *from*, he gives the authority of Captain Parry, who, he says, " has *no doubt* of an open sea to the westward of Melville Island ; as whole fields of ice, interminable to the *sight*, were *observed* to be moving bodily to the westward for days together." Captain Parry may have *told him* so, for aught I know ; but as far as I can find, what he has published in his

Voyage does not seem to me to amount to quite so much as this. At page 86, Captain Parry does, to be sure, say something about a strong *westerly* current, which by-the-by, though perhaps it was only a temporary one, is not much in proof of the existence, *there* at least, of the Reviewer's famous circumvolving current between the Pacific and Atlantic *from* west to east, *if*, as he supposes, there *be* a *passage* for it. But this fact is not at variance with Phoca's circumvolving current in that direction. For *he* does not insist on there positively being a passage for it (though there may be,) any where, but *along the northern shores* of circumpolar lands, *if* it *cannot* pass *between* them, till it rounds the north point of Greenland, and finds its way down its east coast towards the Atlantic. Captain Parry says, " On the 17th September, the current, which for the last two days had been setting to the *westward*, and which could not possibly have escaped our observation had it existed previously to the late westerly and north-westerly gales, was here found to be running stronger than we had before remarked it.—This was made particularly obvious when, having reached the farthest point westward to which we could possibly venture to carry the ships, we were obliged to heave to, in order to watch for an opening that might favor our views ; the ships were at this time drifting to leeward through the water, at the rate of about a mile and a quarter an hour, in spite of which, they went *so fast to the westward* by the land, that Lieutenant Beechey and myself estimated the current to be running at least two miles an hour in *that direction.* I must here remark, that besides the current to which I have now alluded, and by which the floes and heavy masses appeared to be affected, there was, as usual in this navigation, a superficial current also, setting the smaller pieces past the others, at a much quicker rate. Of the causes which now produced this strong *westerly current,* at a time when the contrary might rather have been anticipated, it is of course not easy, with our present limited experience of this part of the Polar Sea, to offer any very probable conjecture; but the impression on our minds, at the time, was, that it was perhaps caused by the *reaction* of the water, which had been forced to the eastward, in the early part of the late gales, *against the ice,* with which the sea was almost entirely covered in that direction. Be this as it may, we did not fail to draw from it one conclusion, which was favorable to the object we had in view, namely, that the drift of so large a body of ice for days together in a westerly direction, indicated a considerable space of open sea *somewhere* in that direction." As to this open space of sea to the westward, it is only necessary to observe here, that as it appears, from other previous remarks, that the tides were here very regular, though it is not made to appear so clear at times, whether the *flood* was from *east* or *west ;* at all events the floating ice was carried by *them,* sometimes one way, and sometimes the other. The currents also are stated, as setting sometimes to the *eastward,* and as such ice must have been carried by *them,* in *that* direction, "the large body of it which was drifting to the *westward,* for days together," might have been only returning back, to fill up the space it had before perhaps occupied there, by means of what Captain Parry calls " the *reaction* of the water, which had been forced to the eastward in the early part of the late gales." In the following year, when Captain Parry had gained more experience in the vicinity of the S.W. extremity of Melville Island, he speaks very differently on the subject of an open sea to the westward of Melville Island. He says : " We had been lying near our present situation, with an easterly wind blowing fresh for thirty-six hours together, and although this was considerably *off* the land, beyond the western point of land now in sight, *the ice had not, during the whole of that time, moved a single yard from the shore ;* affording a *proof* that there *was no space* in which the ice was *at liberty to move to the westward,* and offering a single and striking exception to our former experience." Captain Parry's former experience, however, was not obtained quite so far to the westward, as it was at the time when this single and striking exception occurred.

Captain Ross was instructed "carefully to avoid coming near the coast of America, in order to give it a good offing," for, says the Reviewer, " had it been intended that he should ascertain its position, his instructions, we have no doubt, would have directed him to proceed up the Welcome, and endeavor to pass through Middleton's FROZEN STRAIT ; whereas the object clearly was to avoid being entangled with the *shoals* and *islands* and *ice,* on the *northern shores of America,* which, by the vague accounts of Hearne and Mackenzie, are very similar to the *northern shores* of Siberia." The Reviewer too acknowledged that he had less apprehension of the passage through Behring's Strait being closed against our navigators, except by ice, than of the *difficulties* which they may probably have to encounter on *this side of America.*" No wonder then, if *he* had any influence in the deliberations at the Admiralty, that, in order to avoid *these,* Captain Parry was instructed to proceed by way of Lancaster Sound, and " if it should be found to connect itself with the northern sea, he was to make the best of his way to Behring's Strait;" not at all doubting but that sea would be found free from ice, and navigable the whole way. We have seen the result of that voyage. With that result the Reviewer's resources seem to have failed him, and he very prudently gives up the cudgel to Captain Parry ; and though he seems to have had a *fearful hankering* after *Middleton's Frozen Strait*, or Repulse Bay, which he disbelieved quite as much as he did the existence of Baffin's Bay, yet after what he had said and published he could not well recommend it himself, as a next place of trial. He therefore informs us that " the attempt was to be made as *recommended by Captain Parry*, in a more southern latitude, and *close on the coast of America*." This was preferred to a route through Prince Regent's Inlet, on account of the delay which would necessarily be occasioned by proceeding so far to the northward, as Sir James Lancaster's Sound, in order to get into that inlet.

This last attempt has also failed, but with this " *advantage*" gained, as the Reviewer would say ; that we *now do know* there is such a Bay, as the *Repulse* Bay of Middleton ; and as to " the difficulties which our navigators would probably have to encounter on this side of America," he has been a true prophet for *once*.

And now, as the Reviewer says, " comes the question to be solved as to the best and shortest route to get upon the coast of America. From the appearance and circumstances, at the southern part of Prince Regent's Inlet, there was not a man in the late expedition, who was not convinced that it opened out into the sea, which washes the northern coast of that continent."

This route however did not, it seems, hold out such a fair prospect of success, as that taken last through Hudson's Strait, as the latter was " recommended " by Capt. Parry himself; and the Reviewer " thought it

Data. S

probable that either Hudson's Strait, Sir Thos. Roe's Welcome, or Repulse Bay, or all of them, might afford *navigable passages* into the Polar Sea." These then, with " the knowledge acquired on the former expedition," afforded that " sanguine hope " for the complete solution of " the interesting problem of a north-west passage." The route which last failed, was *then* of course considered " the *best* and shortest, to get upon the coast of America." That by way of Lancaster Sound, and down Prince Regent's Inlet, where the present attempt, it is said, will be made, may therefore be termed the *forlorn hope*, whether it may turn out to be the *best* or not.

As the last expedition failed in reaching the north coast of America, the arguments of the Reviewer and Capt. Parry, in favor of the route along that coast, are of course equally applicable to it in the attempt now to be made there. We will therefore proceed to examine them.

In the first place ; if Capt. Parry should succeed in getting through Prince Regent's Inlet, and to the *southward* of the land forming its *west side ;* and *if* that land should trend nearly on a parallel, so as to be in continuity nearly, or to join *Banks's Land*, he will, in all probability, find just as little difficulty in advancing as far as the west end of that land, along its *southern shore,* as he did to that of Melville Island.

But, if there should *happen* to be a large space to the westward of Banks's Land, *without any land,* and *none between it and the north coast of America,* it is as probable that he will find the whole of that space filled with ices and unnavigable, either to the west or south : and for the same reasons that he could do neither in the whole space between Melville Island and Banks's Land.

But admitting that Capt. Parry should get on the north coast of America, what then ? Why, he says, and the Reviewer also, there " will be a manifest advantage gained, in making the attempt along the northern coast of America, as he will there be certain of a continuity of land. Arrived on the coast of America, and no obstruction from land, *we*," says the Reviewer, " *see no reason* why the passage to Icy Cape, which does not exceed 1500 miles, might not *easily* be accomplished in *one season ;* about 600 of these were actually run on the last voyage in six days ;" but that was *from* the *westward*, quite the *wrong way. He* should have *added*, that " it required five weeks to traverse that distance when going in the opposite direction," *to* the *westward* or *towards* Behring's Strait, as Capt. Parry did. If, as I think, I have shown that there would have been *no advantage* gained by making the passage to the *westward*, along the *northern shores* of the lands extending from Prince Regent's Inlet to Banks's Land, *provided* the North Georgian Islands had *not* existed ; what " manifest advantage," then, can be expected, on the *north* coast of America, *if* there should happen *not* to be lands situated to the northward of it again, along its *whole extent* to Behring's Strait, to keep off those Polar ices, which it is acknowledged by all do, in fact, drift to the southward ? If there should be any extent of it *without* such protection, what is to prevent the advance of such ices, even to that coast ? I may be told that " the summer climate there will be so much warmer," that they will *dissolve* before they reach it. The Reviewer says, " *Supposing* the *theory* of Dr. Brewster to be correct which assigns the greatest degree of cold to the magnetic meridian, the most serious obstruction from ice will probably occur from 90° to 100° of west longitude ; or (setting aside that theory) about midway of the coast, as being the most distant point from the two Oceans; it being well known from experience, that the proximity of a permanently open sea is a circumstance which, of all others, in high latitudes, tends the most to temper the severity of the climate." In this doctrine the Reviewer and Capt. Parry so perfectly agree, that, in speaking of it, they are mutual echoes to each other. But this is only an opinion, a mere assertion, dictated by hope, rather than founded on experience, in a situation so remote from either ocean. The Reviewer "takes for granted," what scarcely admits of a doubt, "that the action of the sun's rays, so much more powerful and radiated from so much more land, along the continuous coast of America, than along the passage discovered by Parry, will produce the same effect of opening a clear channel of water between the coast and the ice," by effecting its dissolution. Capt. Parry says, "Should the sea on the coast of America be found *moderately* deep, and *shelving* towards the shore, (which from the geological character of the known parts of the continent to the south, and of the Georgian Islands to the north, there is reason to believe would be the case, for a considerable distance to the westward,) the facility of navigation would be much increased, on account of the grounding of the *heavy masses* of ice in water sufficiently deep to allow ships to take shelter behind them, at such times as the *floes* close in *upon* the land." Capt. Parry then, it would appear, does not expect much advantage to be gained from the *dissolution* of the ice, as he admits the "heavy masses" may *be there* to take the ground, and "*floes* to close in *upon* the land." He is not so sanguine on this point, therefore, as the Reviewer; nor can Mr. Barrow be, who, having given this subject much of his attention, may be considered *high* authority. He says, at page

373 of his Voyages to the Polar Regions, " In fact, the ice-bergs, and those vast fields of ice which float about on the sea and are *wafted* down by currents into the Atlantic, are chiefly formed on *coasts,* and in *bays,* in *narrow straits,* and at the mouths of great rivers. The whole coast of Siberia is a fertile source of this supply," [on the authority of the Russians I dare say: I wonder what becomes of them all, now the door is shut against them by the land to the northward of Davis's Strait.]

" The multitude of large rivers which fall into the Polar Sea, by carrying down the alluvial earth, have formed numerous and expansive and shallow *bays* of *fresh* water, which in the course of the winter become so many solid masses of ice. As the sources of these rivers, and a great part of their course, are in more southern latitudes, where they never freeze, the water they supply is, in the winter, dammed up near the mouth, and ice-bergs are formed, which, when broken loose, are drifted out to sea. In the same manner the field ice is formed in the *straits,* and bays, and on *shallow coasts,* which, when set afloat in the spring, is *carried out into the sea :* in this situation it is drifted *about* till, heaped piece on piece, and driven *about,* it *again fixes* itself among archipelagos of islands, on *shallow coasts,* and in *straits,* bays, and inlets, where each field becomes a nucleus for an *increasing accumulation,* as in the straits of Belleisle and Behring, for instance, and in *every part of Hudson's Bay* down to the latitude of 50°."

Now, to be sure, if this be the case, there can be *no dissolution* of ices on the north coast of America, and as the wind, it appears, prevails generally *from the northward,* they cannot be carried out to sea in *its teeth ;* so that at this rate, on *such* authority at least, it must be continually encumbered with ices, whether those from the northern ocean find access to it or not. How indeed can such "an increasing accumulation" of ice be dissolved at all, when in Hudson's Bay, so much further to the southward, there is an "increasing accumulation:" nay, even "in the Strait of Belleisle!!" But then the Quarterly Reviewer and Captain Parry will turn round on Mr. Barrow and me, and say, that all this may be so, but "it can scarcely be doubted that the climate on the north coast of America will be found to improve, and the *obstruction* become less, as the ships advance towards the Pacific. Besides, it is well known that the western coast of every continent and large island (even of our own) enjoys a higher temperature by many degrees than the eastern coast in the same parallels of latitude." As a fact, this is true with regard to northern extra tropical continents, whose western coasts have a much higher mean temperature than the eastern. " This difference is extremely striking between the western coast of North America, and the opposite eastern coast of Asia. Mr. Daniel explains it, by the heat evolved in the condensation of vapour swept from the surface of the ocean by the western winds. This general current, in its passage over the land, deposits more and more of its aqueous particles, and by the time that it arrives upon the eastern coasts is extremely dry: as it moves onward, it bears before it the humid atmosphere of the intermediate seas, and arrives upon the opposite shores in a state of saturation. Great part of the vapour is there at once precipitated, and the temperature of the climate raised by the evolution of its latent heat." I apprehend, however, that little of this *effect* will be found to ameliorate the climate on the *north* coast of America much to the eastward of Behring's Strait, owing to the probable proximity and immense quantity of ices to the *north*, from whence frigid winds prevail to counteract it. And therefore that the rule will not perhaps be found so applicable to the eastern and western sides of *Arctic lands*, as it doubtless is to those of extra tropical continents more to the southward. But before the question comes to further proof, which there is much reason to hope it may, by means of the intended *land expedition*, let us try it by the test of the few recorded observations hitherto made on the temperature of the east coast of Greenland, in Hudson's Bay, and Behring's Strait, as *extreme* points in the case. For the first, we will take the authority of Mr. Scoresby, in his Voyage to Greenland, published in 1822, who says, at page 204, after he had landed in Scoresby's Sound : " The heat among the rocks was most oppressive, so much so that my excursion was greatly contracted by the painful languor which the uncommonly high temperature produced. Unfortunately I had no thermometer with me, but I think the temperature could not be below 70° ; to my feelings it was equal to the greatest heat of summer in England." This was on the 25th of July, to the *northward of latitude* 70°. In Hurry's Inlet, he says, " that Mr. Lloyd experienced a degree of heat as oppressive to his feelings as he ever suffered either in the East or West Indies, to which torrid regions he had been a frequent visitor." " It so far overcame some of his men who had attempted to climb an adjoining hill, that they could not proceed, but lying down, fell fast asleep," &c. " The superior heat of the land to that of the sea was most remarkable and striking ; when the temperature on shore was not *less than* 70°, the thermometer *on board the ship*, even near the shore in Scoresby's Sound, never rose, I believe, in the shade above 40°."

The Quarterly Reviewer tells us that, "almost every voyager into Hudson's and Baffin's *Seas* complains of the occasional hot weather and the great annoyance of mosquitoes on the shores. Duncan, when surrounded with ice, had the thermometer in August at 56° in the shade, and 82° in the sun." It is not said what latitude this was in, but it must have been to the *southward of* 65°. So much for the temperature on the eastern side of Greenland and *America*. For that on the west side, and not further north, we will see what Lieutenant Kotzebue found it to be in Behring's Strait, and also in the *shallow sound* bearing his name, which being *almost surrounded* by land, may very naturally be expected to have the temperature of its water, as well as that of the atmosphere, considerably *raised* by the radiation of heat from it. On the 26th of July, when near the St. Lawrence Islands (situated to the *southward* of Behring's Strait, and between Asia and America,) and in latitude 63° N. the temperature of the air was 53° 8′, and of the surface of the sea, 41° 2′. In Kotzebue Sound, in lat. 63½° and long. 162°, from the 2d to the 13th of August, the *mean* temperature of the air was about 63°, and that of the sea water about 52°. On the 19th of August, in latitude 66° 16′ N. and a little to the northward of East Cape, the temperature of the air was 44°, and the sea water 35° 8′. These few facts will not lead any one in his senses to conclude that the *waters of the Pacific*, which at the surface are of a temperature of 70° or 80°, could possibly have *composed any* of the fluid *here*. Neither do they prove that the climate of the western coast of America is "higher by many degrees than the eastern," at least on equal parallels, though *somewhat* higher in latitude 68° than 70° on the east side of *Greenland*.

This *western* part of America, forming the east side

of Behring's Strait ought of course, according to the rule of the Reviewer and Captain Parry, to be the warmest part of it on an equal parallel. Yet, being of so low a temperature as it appears to be, on what ground can it be believed that there will be a better climate further to the *eastward*, on the *north* coast, than there is here? Nay, by *their own rule*, must it not be *progressively colder* from Icy Cape all the way *to their point* of *greatest frigidity* and obstruction, about " midway of the coast?" Or to the one supposed by Dr. Brewster to be " situated in about 80° N. latitude and 100° W. longitude?"

I must, however, take the liberty of borrowing one of the Reviewer's own arguments to prove, that the climate " from midway," on the north coast of America, towards the Pacific, can *not* be milder than it has been experienced at its western extremity.

In the beginning of the year 1818, he took much pains to show that the temperature of our climate in England was *lower* in the three summer months of 1816 and 1817, by from 11° to 20°, than it had been in corresponding months of 1805, 1806, and 1807—that " the remarkable chilliness of the atmosphere, in the summer months of those two years, was owing to the *appearance* of ice in the Atlantic"—that " it would be a waste of words to enter into any discussion on the diminution of temperature, which *must necessarily* be occasioned by the *proximity* of vast mountains, and islands of ice;" in short, that the westerly winds *did* in fact acquire an unusually *frigorific character*, by having passed over a few icebergs drifting to the southward in the Atlantic, at the distance of some hundreds of miles from the British Isles. What then must be the character of winds in the circumpolar

Data.   T

Arctic sea, *if* they "prevail generally from the *north* ?"
And what *their* influence on the climate of the whole
north coast of America, *upon which* they blow, and the
ice drifts ; it being *a lee shore ?* That the winds, judging
theoretically, should prevail from the northward in the
Arctic regions, is perhaps indisputable ; and, though the
Reviewer has admitted it to be so, yet it is as well to
establish the fact by the testimony of navigators in that
quarter of the globe.

Mr. Scoresby, from a mean of nine years' observation
in the Spitzbergen sea, in the months of April and
May, has "estimated the frigid winds passing over ice,
to be in proportion to the mild winds blowing from the
sea, as 173 N. to 69 S." In Baffin's Bay, it appears
by Captain Ross's register, that the northerly winds
were in proportion to the southerly, as 75 to 59—the
easterly and westerly, as 62 E. to 65 W.—And on an
examination of Captain Parry's register of the winds
for 448 days between July 1819, and September 1820,
the northerly winds were in proportion to the southerly,
as 316 N. to 140 S. ; and the easterly to the westerly,
as 118 E. to 245 W. or thereabouts. So that *if* any
ice be either formed along the *north coast* of America,
or drive down upon it by these winds, " prevailing, as
they do, from the northward and westward," and a
Polar current from the same quarter, I should like to
know by what possible means it can be expected to be
cleared of it, *except* by the effect of *heat ?* Or, if that
which perhaps may be so dissolved is, as I believe,
replaced constantly, though probably imperceptibly, by
the *tendency* of the whole body to *move southward*, (whether it extends five or ten or any number of degrees
to the northward, towards the Pole,) how that *north*
coast, or the north or west coasts of any lands, on any

parallels and meridians between the N.W. part of Greenland and Melville Island, can be otherwise than perpetually encumbered with ice, *provided no other land be between them and the Pole?* But more especially so, if we admit also the effect of the Reviewer's circumvolving current from the Pacific, to be " rushing in" through Behring's Strait with " the greatest velocity :" for as that current is *bound to the Atlantic*, it must set to the eastward from thence, and carry along with it floating masses of ice.

Lieutenant Kotzebue says : " The direction of the current was always N.E. in Behring's Strait, and stronger on the Asiatic than on the American coast. I estimate the current on the Asiatic coast in the channel, at the greatest depth, to be three miles an hour, when the wind blew fresh from the south. The constant N.E. direction of the current in Behring's Strait proves that the water meets with no obstruction, and consequently a passage must exist, though perhaps not adapted to navigation :" and believing, in consequence of what our Quarterly Reviewer had told him, that the current in Baffin's Bay runs to the south, he thought " no doubt can remain that the mass of water which flows into Behring's Strait takes its course round America, and returns through Baffin's Bay into the ocean."—Mr. Von Chamisso, the naturalist, who was with Kotzebue in the Rurick, is not quite so positive, nor so sanguine: for he says, " After we had *tried to prove* that a current goes to the north through Behring's Strait, we must *confess* that it is *too weak*, and can force but too little water through the narrow entrance, to correspond with those currents which flow from Dävis's Strait, and along the east coast of Greenland, towards the south." This gentleman too, it seems, believed, at the time he wrote this, in the Reviewer's current down

" Baffin's Sea," which we have seen had no existence but in his own fertile imagination.

Captain Burney supposed " the current in Behring's Strait to be periodical ; were it perpetual," said he, " its moderate rate through a channel neither wide nor deep, could contribute little towards a current in the Greenland seas." Very little, truly—and perhaps has nothing to do with the current in the Spitzbergen sea. We have seen, from the testimony of Mr. Scoresby junior, that the current there *is perpetual.* Indeed, from the united testimony of hundreds besides, there can be no doubt of the fact of a constant current from the northward, out of the Polar Sea, towards the Atlantic Ocean : and because it is exactly such an effect as must of necessity result from physical causes originating in heat and cold on the globe. This, too, being the *only* effect of that cause hitherto discovered in the Arctic regions, has appeared to me to be, of all others, the strongest argument against the practicability at least—nay, almost the existence of a passage for ships from the Atlantic into (what I understand by) the Polar Sea, on *any* parallel and meridian, *from the N.W. part of Greenland to Melville Island.* The space between Melville Island and the coast of America, to Behring's Strait, still remains to be explored by *ships.* To that space the same argument is applicable under the like circumstances. For, should a similar effect (the certain result of the same cause) *not* be found there, the same conclusion must follow—Impracticability.

But further, even if such similar current should be hereafter discovered flowing from the Polar Sea, somewhere within that space, towards the Atlantic, between insulated lands ; it may indeed prove the existence of a passage, perhaps under the ice, for water

and fish, like that between Melville Island and Banks's
Land, without proving its practicability for ships.   Because, as such current must of necessity be from the
north or west, or both, it will in all probability close
up the narrower passages with ice.   Even admitting
then the circumvolving current of the Reviewer (not
from the *Pacific*, but) from Behring's Strait to the eastward, to be flowing towards the Atlantic by way of
channels yet unexplored between Melville Island and
the coast of America, if these channels should not
be sufficiently wide to allow the heavier masses and
fields of ice to pass through with the current, from the
northward, or westward, or both ; the natural consequence, I should apprehend, must be an accumulation
of icy obstruction at the *northern* and *western* openings
of such channels ; as was the case in the space between
the west end of Melville Island and Banks's Land, and
since that time, in the Strait of the Fury and Hecla.
And this, too, on the same principle, and for the same
reason, that a grating placed across a stream would
cause an accumulation of such *floating* substances as
could not pass through it, on the side *next its source.*

At the same time, it must be observed, that even the
future proof of such current from the northward or
westward, from the Polar Sea, or along the northern
coast of America, will not in the least tend to prove
that either the one or the other *has the waters* of the
Pacific Ocean for its *source*, as has been so wildly conjectured : for the waters of that ocean can have no
more to do with it, as a *cause* of its *existence* in *any part*
of the north circumpolar regions, (except through the
medium of evaporation and a northerly movement in
the atmosphere,) than the man in the moon.

I have not yet been able to learn whether any current from the westward, of a permanent character, was met with under the ice, in the Strait of Fury and Hecla. But if there was, it may be considered (according to the view I have taken of the subject) as a circumstance unfavorable to success.

There is another fact mentioned in the Appendix to Captain Franklin's account of his journey to the mouth of the Copper-Mine River, which tends to prove that the climate to the *westward* of the meridian (113° 6′) of Fort Enterprise, is *colder* than that to the eastward of it. He says, " The easterly winds predominate in the country to the northward of the Great Slave Lake; and whilst they blow, the weather *is milder* than *during the westerly winds.* The *coldest,* and I may add the strongest wind, in every season, in this country, is the *north-west.*"

Now, if the westerly winds in the summer months of 1816 and 1817 were so remarkably chilled, in their way to our shores, by passing over a few icebergs in the Atlantic, as to reduce the temperature of the climate of Great Britain from 11 to 20 degrees, the Reviewer can have no objection, I presume, to admit that the westerly winds to the northward of the Great Slave Lake must have come from a *colder* climate, *westward* of the 113th meridian, than that could possibly be to the *eastward* of it, from *whence* the winds, Captain Franklin says, were *milder.* In short, that *they* were *frigified* too, somewhere and somehow, on their passage. And as ice was the cause of the unusual chilliness of our westerly winds here, by the Reviewer's own argument, therefore, the colder character of the westerly and north-westerly winds, to the northward of the Great Slave Lake, must have been owing to the same cause too; the abundance of ice in the direction from whence these winds came. And as even *westerly* winds had this cold character, some of this ice, it may be supposed, was as far to the southward as the coast of America: for on a flat shelving shore, such as parts of the " north coast may be, it is impossible to pre-scribe how far inland low field ice shall not be driven by the pressure of other ice, forced by tempestuous weather towards the land." Captain Burney also ob-serves, " that the shallowness of the sea near the north coast of Asia, the freshes discharged into it from many large rivers, and the coast fronting the north, render it more liable to be frozen, than the seas of Greenland and Spitzbergen in a much higher latitude. The northern lands in the Icy Sea are impediments to the *dispersion* of ice, and hence arises the great difficulty of navigation in that sea." This passage is partly appli-cable likewise to the north coast of America. But Captain Franklin has recorded his favorable opinion of the practicability of a passage for ships along that coast. " Our researches," he says, " as far as they have gone, seem to favor the opinion of those who con-tend for the practicability of a N.W. passage. The general line of coast probably runs east and west, nearly in the latitude assigned to the Mackenzie river, the Sound into which Kotzebue entered, and Re-pulse Bay; and very little doubt can, in my opi-nion be entertained of the existence of a continued sea in or about *that line of direction*. A connexion with Hudson's Bay is rendered more probable from the same kind of fish abounding on the coast we visited, and on the coast to the north of the Churchill river. The portion of sea over which we passed is navigable

for ships of any size; the ice we met with, particularly
after quitting Detention Harbour, would not have arrested a strong boat. The chain of islands affords
shelter from all heavy seas, and there are good harbours
at convenient distances."

There can be no doubt that the chain of islands
seen to the northward of that portion of the coast explored by Capt. Franklin, from the Copper Mine River
eastward, would shelter ships from heavy seas, if it
were likely there could be any produced there. And
the shelter those nearest, as well as the North Georgian
Islands, afforded to that part of the coast, was the reason why it was not much encumbered with ice, more
especially to the eastward of Detention Harbour; as
George the Fourth's Coronation Gulf is almost completely protected by Wilmot's Chain, and other islands
to the northward of it. If a similar chain should
exist from Cape Hearne to Icy Cape, there will probably be a navigable passage all the way between it and
the coast of America, provided it runs, as Capt. Franklin supposes, east and west, nearly in the latitude assigned to the Mackenzie River, and the Sound into
which Kotzebue entered. But there is some reason to
fear that the coast of America, *westward* of Mackenzie's
River, will be found to trend more to the northward
than the dotted imaginary line of direction so arbitra-
rily assigned to it by geographers. The late Admiral
Burney said, "an account or notice is given by Kobilef of a great river, in the coast of America, to the *north
of Behring's Strait*, which river is described to take a
long course in a southerly direction, and its banks to
be full of villages." Can the Sound discovered by
Lieut. Kotzebue to the northward of Behring's Strait,
between Capes Krusenstern and Espenberg, lead to

this great river, " described to take a long course in a *southerly* direction?" Though Kotzebue's detail of his proceedings in this Sound is rather obscure and un-satisfactory, and so apparently contradictory, in some parts, as to implant a doubt of its correctness; yet I am rather disposed to attribute this to the translation, which is evidently defective, than to any intention on his part, to conceal known facts, for the purpose of deception. He entered this Sound, named after him, on the 1st of August. " At 11 o'clock (he says) we were at the entrance of a broad inlet; the coast va-nished in the east, and high mountains showed them-selves in the north." Here the wind abated, and he anchored in seven fathoms water, in lat. 66° 42′ 30″, and long. 164° 12′ 50″: at 7 o'clock he weighed again, "and steered to the eastward (*across*, but as he says) up the strait." " On the 2nd, at day-break, our ex-pectations were at the highest pitch; there was still nothing but open sea to the east." The next passage is rather remarkable. " As we now saw low land in the south, the direction of which was likewise to the east, we could no longer doubt that we were really in a broad channel, as we always continued to see the open sea in the east." Now, if there be any channel leading to the eastward, it must be opposite to his noon position of this day, which was in lat. 66° 35′ 8″, and long. 162° 19′, in 8 fathoms water, where he says he was " obliged to tack, *because* the wind *turned to the S.E.*" But if there had been a passage to the *eastward*, where he says " the sea continued open," surely the shifting of the wind, in soundings of eight fathoms, need not have prevented him from standing on in that direction, on the starboard tack, to explore an *open space* in so *promising* a quarter, or at least till he had seen the land

Data.   U

in continuity, or had shoaled his water, so as not to be able to proceed further. *According* to his published *Chart* of this Sound, however, the land *must have been seen* to the eastward, from the noon position of the Rurick on the 2d August; for the whole eastern side of Kotzebue's Sound is delineated *in continuity,* and a working track along it is laid down as far to the southward as Chamisso Island. He anchored to the westward of this island, "in eight fathoms water, in an opening five miles broad, where he still cherished the hope of discovering a passage into the Frozen Ocean;" which hope, it may therefore be presumed, had *thus far* been *disappointed,* and as it also was *here.* "The anchor was weighed; we sailed (to the eastward) up the Strait, and when we had passed the narrow part, we again cast anchor in seven fathoms." He then proceeded to examine the coast eastward with his boats; and on the 7th, when in Eschscholtz Bay, he says, "We had advanced so far at noon, that we could *distinctly observe* that the *land was united every where.* At the distance of a full mile from the shore, the water had decreased to the depth of *five feet,* and the hope of discovering *a river* also *vanished.*" But he says, further on: "I called the Bay after our physician, Eschscholtz. I do not doubt that there *was* a river behind the high mountains, which the shoals, however, would not permit us to investigate. The ebb tide runs out seven, and the flood only five hours. They change regularly; the current sets with more violence *out* than in, and sometimes runs two knots." These are *indications* of a *river,* but not of a channel leading to a sea; but Kotzebue, in his *Chart,* has connected the whole coast round Eschscholtz and Spafariefs Bays, though it does not seem quite certain that he carefully examined the latter:

for on the 10th August he says, " We left Eschscholtz
Bay with a fresh S.E. wind. I now wished to examine the land to the south. It lay at the distance of
seven miles from us:" but his track in the ship is further
off, leading towards Cape Deceit, in a direct line nearly
from Chamisso Island. However, he says, that " he
steered along the coast W.S.W. because he considered
the examination of the *east unnecessary ;* as he had *distinctly seen* the *connexion* of the land from the point of
Chamisso Island." Whether he alludes, in this passage,
to the *south* part of the Sound *eastward* from Cape Deceit, round to Chamisso Island, or the east coast itself of the Sound, from abreast of the noon position
2d August, southward to the point next to Chamisso Island, it is rather difficult to say, but not very
material.

Mr. Barrow, in mentioning this subject in his account
of Voyages to the Arctic Regions, says, " Kotzebue
entered an inlet in latitude about $67\frac{1}{2}$ to 68°. Its extent
to the eastward was not determined; but the Rurick
proceeded in that direction as far as the meridian of
160°, which corresponds with that of Norton Sound."
From the Indians " Lieut. Kotzebue learned, that at the
bottom of the inlet was a *strait*, through which there
was a passage into the great sea ; and that it required
nine days rowing in one of their boats to reach this
sea. This, Kótzebue *thinks*, must be the great
northern Ocean, and that the whole of the land to the
northward of the inlet must either be an island, or
an archipelago of islands." From what Lieutenant
Kotzebue has *published*, it does not appear that what
he learned from the Indians was in the least connected
with any " *strait* at the *bottom* of the *inlet*," or on the
eastern side of the Sound ; but referred to one situated
on the *western* side, in the Bay of Good Hope, between

Capes Deceit and Espenberg. Kotzebue says, he
went in his boats, on the 12th of August, to examine
this strait. " After proceeding about four miles," says
he, " we arrived at a Cape where the land suddenly
took a direction from south to west. From a hill I
observed a broad arm to the west, which ran from the
sea into the land, and there wandered in several
windings between the mountains." Here, meeting with
an old Indian, " I took much pains," says he, " to
make my American comprehend, that I wished to
know how far this branch might extend ? He at
last comprehended me, and made me understand his
answer, by the following pantomime : he seated himself
on the ground, and rowed eagerly with his arms ; this
business he interrupted *nine* times, closing his eyes as
many times, and resting his head on his hand. *I learnt*
by *this* that it would take *nine days* to get to the open
sea, through this branch." And, a few pages further on,
Kotzebue says, " the account given by the American
may be correct, and this branch either extends to Norton Sound, or joins Schischmareff's Bay." Now, as
Norton Sound lies to the *southward*, and Schischmareff Bay to the *westward* of the place Kotzebue was
examining, the " Great Sea" to which this strait or
branch led, must have been in one or other of *those directions.* How then could Kotzebue have " *thought* it
must have been the Great *Northern* Ocean, that the Indians informed him it required nine days rowing to
reach ?" He does indeed say, afterwards, when speaking of Kotzebue Sound, " I certainly hope that *this*
sound may lead to important discoveries next year ; and
though a north-east passage may not with certainty be
depended on, yet I believe *I shall be able* to penetrate
much further to the *east,* as the land has very deep in-
dentures." Mr. Von Chamisso, who accompanied

Lieutenant Kotzebue, in his "remarks," has this passage : " We observe that that part of the American coast
which we examined to the north of Behring's Strait,
appeared to us to excite the hope of finding a channel
among the entrances and friths which intersect it, and
which might lead to the Icy Sea towards the mouth of
Mackenzie River, without doubling Icy Cape, which
would then be part of an island ;" and in a foot note,
he adds : " Several Journals have published a letter
from the author of these articles (San Francisco, New
California, on the 28th of October 1816,) in which this
opinion was delivered ; an error of the copyist has
altered the sense, so as to make it seem as if *this
entrance had really been examined by us."* These passages
seem to afford some ground to suspect that there may
be an opening on the east side of Kotzebue Sound which
had been *seen*, but *not examined ;* or on what can Kotzebue have founded his belief, that he should "be able to
penetrate much further to the *east*" the following year?
Certainly, from what he has *said*, concerning the bottom
of that sound, and an inspection of the *chart* he has
published, if true, no such belief or even hope can be
excited ; for he has connected the land completely
round it, with the exception of the strait in the Bay
of Good Hope, *leading* to the *westward.* Willing to
believe him to be an officer of honorable principles and
veracity, I can hardly bring myself to suppose him otherwise without further proof. The hope he expressed, (if
he really had any,) of being "able to penetrate further to
the east" out of Kotzebue Sound, must have rested on
the known existence of some strait *supposed* to lead from
the east side of that sound to the Northern Ocean.
And if what he learned from the Indians did refer to
such a strait, instead of the one on the *west side*, as it

evidently does both in his chart and publication, he may inadvertently have told the truth to Mr. Barrow on his arrival in London, and afterwards have been commanded by his government to falsify both. However, I must confess, I would much rather attribute this discordance to some misunderstanding, than allow myself to suppose the other to be even possible. If, on the other hand, there is only a river at the bottom of Eschscholtz Bay, " behind the mountains, which the shoals would not permit Kotzebue to investigate," it could hardly be expected to communicate with the NORTHERN Ocean, unless by another branch. In that case, it would not answer to the description of the "Great River" mentioned by Kobilef, which is said " to take a long course in a *southerly* direction." *If*, therefore, any such river exist, it must be looked for still further to the northward, and perhaps beyond Icy Cape.

From some facts stated in the account of Captain Parry's attempt through Lancaster Sound, and in Captain Franklin's Journey, it seems *doubtful* whether what may be *properly* termed the Polar Sea has yet been reached. But it is very *possible* that each may have navigated in waters separated from it by continuity of land, at some yet undefined distance to the northward and westward ; in which waters, the North Georgian Islands, and others perhaps to the westward of them, are situated, and extend perhaps as far as the 130th meridian; and into which both the Coppermine and Mackenzie's rivers disembogue : in short, a mediterranean sea, communicating with the Bays of Hudson and Baffin, by various channels, through which the flood tide finds its way from the Atlantic and Spitzbergen Sea.

Captain Ross found the flood tide to set *from* the

southward all the way up the east side of Baffin's Bay. The rise and fall decreased gradually, and the times of high-water at full and change were *later*, as far as he advanced to the *northward*. The tide of flood set to the southward and westward on the west side of that Bay, as he returned along it, to the southward.

Captain Parry, near Possession Bay, in lat. 73° 31′ 16″, and long. 77° 22′, says, "he found the rise and fall of tide, as nearly as could be judged from the marks on the beach, to befrom 6 to 8 feet. While the tide was rising, the stream came from the northward and westward along the shore of the Bay. It is more than probable, therefore, that the flood comes from the N.W. on this part of the coast." Whether the flood came from the west, out of Lancaster Sound, or from the northward down the west side of Baffin's Bay, it must of course, *at this place*, have taken the direction imposed on it by the trending of the coast from Cape Liverpool towards the south-east.

On the 7th of August, when in Prince Regent's Inlet, off Port Bowen, he says, "The whole rise of tide (being nearly the highest of the springs,) appears to have been TEN feet. The *ebb* was found to set strong *to the southward* in shore. A boat being moored to the bottom, at three miles' distance from the land, at 5 P.M., not the smallest current was perceptible. From these and several subsequent observations, there is good reason to suppose that the *flood tide* comes from the *southward* in this inlet." Captain Parry adds: "I have before observed, that the east and west coasts which form this grand inlet are probably islands: and on an inspection of the chart, I think it will also appear highly probable that a communication will one day be found to exist between this inlet and Hudson's Bay, either through the broad unexplored channel called Sir' Thomas Roe's Welcome, or through Repulse Bay, which has not yet been satisfactorily examined. It is also probable that a channel will be found to exist, between the western land and the northern coast of America; *in which case*, the flood-tide which came from the southward, may have proceeded round the *southern* part of the *west land* out of the Polar Sea: part of it setting up the inlet, and part down the Welcome, according to the testimony of all the old navigators." That the east and west lands forming Prince Regent's Inlet may be islands, is very likely; and that it communicates with Hudson's Bay, appears to be little less than *certain :* for (to my mind at least,) it is *proved* by the flood-tide running from the southward.

As I believe *this tide* has its source in the *south* and *east*, and that it flows from the Atlantic and Spitzbergen Sea, through Hudson's, Cumberland, and Davis's Straits, by channels of communication with them all, and perhaps by others yet unexplored, still further to the northward on the west side of Baffin's Bay, *that* in Prince Regent's Inlet is consequently a part of it. This part, when it reaches the north entrance of Prince Regent's Inlet, naturally takes the direction of the east and west lands forming it ; setting to the eastward on the former, and to the westward along the latter towards the Wellington Channel ; and making the times of high-water, at full and change, progressively *later* in *that* direction, as far as, or perhaps beyond Melville Island: the other part of the great general flood sets down the Welcome, along the *west* side of Hudson's Bay, as it naturally must, from the trending of the yet known land, and making the times of high-water at full and change, on *that coast*, progressively *later* to the *southward*. This fact, therefore, can by no means prove, as Ellis and others have concluded, that because the flood-tide in the Welcome sets to the *southward*, it must necessarily come from the *west, originally*, out of the Polar Sea, and that *therefore* there must be a navigable passage. Nor, indeed, if the flood tide shall hereafter be found to come from the westward, along the southern shores of the land west of Prince Regent's Inlet, will it in the least prove that the *Polar Sea* is its grand *source*, as has been conjectured. For the same fact would occur in an inclosed sea, by the flood taking the direction of its circumbounding land. It will no doubt prove the existence of a channel between *that land* west of Prince Regent's Inlet and the northern coast of America, but nothing more.

Channels of communication are *known* to exist between the Atlantic and Baffin's and Hudson's Bays, and now, there perhaps can be little doubt of one between them by way of Lancaster Sound, and Prince Regent's Inlet. There probably are others, though yet undiscovered.

As far as can be gathered from the experience of Captain Parry, and the facts stated by him as well as Mr. Fisher, in their respective publications, it would appear that the flood-tide through Lancaster Sound, and Barrow's Strait, all the way to Melville Island, has its *general* flow, *not* from the *west*, but from the *east*, and from the northward between some of the North Georgian Islands. The times of high water, too, at full and change, as far as they can be got at, seem to have been progressively *later* from *east to west*, and the rise and fall of tide was also less and less in *that direction*. On the 22d of August, when off Gascoyne Inlet, about the longitude of 96°, Mr. Fisher says, " I have only to add one circum-

Data.   X

stance which I feel less pleasure in relating; it is that we found the *ebb-tide come* from the *westward;* the tide ebbed during the time we were on shore, which was about fifty minutes, between 10 and 11 inches." On the 28th of August, when off Point Gilman, Captain Parry says, "The tide was *rising* by the shore from noon till half past 4, P.M. at which time the boats left the beach, and by the high-water mark, it was considered probable that it would rise an hour longer. The time of high water may therefore be taken at half past 5, which will make that of full and change about 12 o'clock. Mr. Ross found, on rowing round the point near which he landed, that the stream was setting strong against him from the northward. We had tried the current (tide) in the offing at noon," (in lat. 75° 3′ 12″, and long. 103° 34′ 37″) " by mooring the small boat to the bottom, when it was found to run in a south direction, at the rate of half a mile per hour. At 4 P.M., near the same station, it was setting *S.S.W.* ⅝ of a mile per hour, so that it would appear tolerably certain, that the *flood-tide* here comes from the *northward*." On the 2d of September, in lat. 74° 58, and long. 107° 3′ 31″, Captain Parry says, "When the boats landed at 1. 40. P. M. the tide had fallen a foot by the shore. It continued to *fall* till 7 P.M. and then rose again, the whole fall of tide not exceeding *five,* or *five* and a *half feet.* At the time we landed, Lieutenant Beechey tried for a current in the offing, but could find none. At half past 7 the tide was setting E.N.E. at the rate of a mile and a half an hour, and at a quarter before ten, after I returned on board, it was still setting slowly to the *eastward.* By the above observations, the time of high water at full and change of the moon seems to be about ¾ *after one o'clock.* The direction of the tide of flood does not appear so clear."

" *If,*" says Captain Parry, " it come from the westward, there must be a tide and half tide, but it seems *more probable,* on an inspection of the chart, that here, as on the eastern side of Byam Martin's Island, it will be found to come from the northward between the islands." But it is *most* probable, that, as the tide setting *to the E.N.E.* at half past 7 *was the ebb,* the flood must have set to the *W.S.W.* in the *same place,* unless Captain Parry can give any good reason why it should *not.*

On the 6th of September, in lat. 74° 47′, and long. 110° 34′, Captain Parry says, " It was low water by the shore at half past 9, and it had risen between two and three feet when the boats came away at half past 12. During this time, the ships were tending to a *tide coming* strong *from the eastward, from which direction* it is therefore probable" (why not *certain ?*) "that the *flood tide* runs on this part of the *coast,* though we had no opportunity of trying its true set in the offing." Again, on the 9th of September, "Considering our present detention so near the shore a good opportunity of observing the true rise and fall of the tides, I caused a pole to be fixed on the beach for the purpose, by which it was found to be high water at half past 4 o'clock in the morning, and the tide *ebbed* till half past 10. From this time till half past 4 P.M. when it was again high water, the tide had risen *two feet eight inches ;* so that, small as this tide was, it seems to be very regular. The direction of the stream of flood was, as usual, not so easy to determine. But I shall give the facts as they occurred. At the time of *low water* by the shore, and for an hour and a quarter *before* it took place, the current was setting to the *eastward* at the rate of three quarters of a mile per hour. It continued to run thus for the greater part of the day, but at *times* it was observed to set in an opposite direction, and now and

then no current whatever was perceptible. From 8 till 11
P.M. it was running strong to the westward, after which
it stopped, and then began to set the ice the contrary
way. I have been thus minute in mentioning the above
particulars, not with a hope of throwing any light upon
that interesting question of the direction of the tides in
this part of the Polar Sea, but to show how impossible
it is, with the land close on one side, and on the other
innumerable masses of ice, in almost constant motion,
to arrive at any *satisfactory conclusion* on the subject. In
Winter Harbour, in lat. 74° 47′ 15″, and long. 110°
48′ 30″, it was found to be high water at 29 minutes past
1 o'clock, and the mean rise and fall was only 2 feet 7
inches." On the 1st of August, in the year following,
when Captain Parry was released from Winter Harbour,
and had rounded Cape Hearne, he says, " We found the
ships to be considerably impeded by a tide *or current*
setting to the eastward, which, as it slacked about 7 in
the evening, I considered to be the flood, the time of high
water at Winter Harbour, this day, being about half
past 7." In this instance, as in others, where a *supposed*
flood tide from the westward has been mentioned, it is
coupled with an expression of some *doubt* as to its being
a tide *or* current. The flood tide from the *eastward* has
been stated *more decidedly.* Why, in this case and at
this place, Captain Parry should have considered the
flood to come from the *westward*, merely because this
" tide *or current* slacked about the time it was high
water in Winter Harbour;" when not very far from the
same place, on the 6th of September of the former year,
he thought that the tide coming from the *eastward* was
probably *the flood*, he can of course assign some good
reason. It seems to me, however, that this stream was
most probably a *current*, especially as he says on the

14th of August, "The frequent experience we had of the quickness with which currents are thus formed, in consequence, merely, of the wind setting the various bodies of ice in motion, naturally leads us to this useful caution, that one or two trials of the set of the stream in icy seas must not be too hastily assumed in drawing any conclusions as to its constant or periodical direction." This observation may be truly applicable to temporary *currents*, but not to tides, which, though they may be accelerated or retarded in their velocity by various causes, must always set in the direction imposed on them by others of locality, which cannot vary, the trendings of the lands between which they have their course. Upon the whole, it appears that Captain Parry then did find the rise and fall of tide to be less to the *west* than to the *eastward* and *southward, from whence* therefore, a *probable*, at least, if not a "satisfactory, general" conclusion may be drawn, that the flood tide *comes originally*.

Though we cannot come at the *direction* of the flood tide on that part of the coast of America which Capt. Franklin travelled and coasted, yet at the mouth of the Copper-Mine River, in lat. 67° 48′ and long. 114° 37′, he states, that a "rise and fall of *four inches* in the water was observed." This was the *farthest west* and the *least* observed. In travelling from thence along the coast to the *eastward*, the rise and fall, though very small, it appears, did *increase ;* from whence, therefore, it may be fairly *argued* that the flood *comes*, till the contrary shall be *proved*. In about 112° west, Capt. Franklin says, "For the last two days the water rose and fell about nine inches. The tides, however, seemed to be very irregular, and we could not determine the direction of the ebb or flood. A current, setting to the eastward, was running about two miles an hour during

our stay." About the mouth of Banks River, Capt.
Franklin says, "at this place the water fell *two feet*
during the night ;" and on the 3d and 4th of August, in
Bathurst Inlet, he observed "a fall of *more* than *two
feet* in the water during the night." On the 15th of
August he adds, "it may here be remarked that we
observed the first *regular* return of the tides in Warren-
der's and Parry's Bays, but their set could not be
ascertained. The rise of water did not amount to more
than *two feet*." Now it must be remarked that War-
render Bay is about the *easternmost* limit of Capt.
Franklin's researches.

Though I will not go so far as to say that the foregoing facts, which I have collected chiefly from the
publications "of those who contend for the practicability of a N.W. passage," tend to disprove it; yet, they
are evidently very *strong indications* of an extensive
Mediterranean Sea, such as I have supposed may exist,
having communication by various channels with the
Bays of Hudson and Baffin, though not with the *Polar
Sea proper*.

Though the Quarterly Reviewer says, " Hearne talks
vaguely of the sea being full of islands at the mouth of
the Copper-Mine River, as far as he could see with a
good pocket telescope ;" yet Capt. Franklin has proved
him to be quite correct, with regard to the *numerous
islands ;* and perhaps it may fall to *his* lot, also, to prove,
whether or not Hearne was as correct too, in "thinking it more than probable, that the Copper-Mine River
empties itself into a sort of inland sea, or extensive
bay, somewhat like that of Hudson." There is another
circumstance yet to be mentioned, which goes far to
show, that Hearne may be right in his judgment; at
least it seems so to me. On the 17th and 18th of Octo-

ber, when Capt. Parry was at Melville Island, "the deer were observed in vast numbers, preparatory to their departure *over the ice* to the coast of America, after which one or two only were seen." The Quarterly Reviewer says, on the return of summer, " it was quite astonishing to behold the rapidity with which the various plants of the island pushed forth their leaves and flowers, the moment the snow was off the ground. Whether it was the abundance of these flowers that tempted the *musk oxen* and *rein-deer* to make the long journey *over the ice*, or whether they came to these secluded and *peaceable* islands to drop their young, is not known. In a valley, formed by the stream of a ravine, which had the same lively appearance as that of an English meadow, a whole herd of musk oxen were seen grazing; and our surprise (says Capt. Parry) in some degree ceased, at the immense distance which these animals must travel in the course of their *annual visits* to these dreary and desolate regions; as such a pasture, affording undisturbed and luxuriant feeding during the summer months, may, in spite of the general appearance of the island, hold out sufficient induce-ment for their annual emigration;" and the Quarterly Reviewer says in another place, that " deer migrate from America to Melville Island, which is upwards of 300 miles from the Continent." Capt. Franklin too, in his Appendix, No. 5, at page 668, informs us that " in summer the musk oxen migrate in considerable num-bers from the Continent (America) to the various islands which exist in the Polar Sea," so that the fact is stated and, of course, *believed* by *all* these authorities. In the autumn these animals pass from Melville Island to the coast of America. In the spring, nay in the " summer" too, they return to that island, and " various " others

" which exist in the Polar Sea." Now by what means
are they enabled to make these long journeys? Not
by land ; for those, who suppose the navigable passage
to exist, which is now once more to be sought for between Melville Island and the north coast of America,
cannot believe there *is land* any where in *continuity,*
in that space, for them to travel *on.* Not by water; for
though those whose trade it is to feed curiosity with a
goose's quill, know that there is no lack of credulity
among us, whatever there may be of faith : yet, I
presume they would find it somewhat difficult to
make any *John Bull* believe that these deer and musk
oxen swim the distance of 300 miles twice a year!
Well then, unless these beasts " take unto themselves
wings and fly," to pass " *over the ice,*" they must of
course make their long journeys *upon* it. If so, it
may be supposed to be continuous, and almost permanent, or they could hardly migrate thus upon it,
not only in the spring and autumn, but even the
summer.

The medium however, let it be what it may, which
enables these animals to do this, would not, I suppose,
be the very *best* for *ships* to *sail in ;* and therefore, *if* the
fact of their migration be true, as thus stated, it cannot
but render the hope of a navigable passage rather forlorn. But if that medium *should happen* to be land, it
must be land in continuity, which would at once decide
the question of the existence of a N. W. passage in the
negative.

In that case, the result would be the same, whether
an attempt at the discovery should be made from *this*
side, or from Behring's Strait. But why those " who
contend for the existence and practicability of a N.W.
passage for ships," should prefer the former, has ap-

peared to me quite unaccountable. Captain Parry, however, has recorded *his* reasons, such as they are, in its favor, in these words. " In the course of the foregoing narrative, it may have been remarked that the westerly and north-westerly winds were always found to produce the effect of *clearing* the *southern* shores of the new Georgian Islands of *ice*, while they always brought with them clear weather, which is essentially necessary in prosecuting discoveries in such navigation. *This* circumstance, together with the fact of our having *sailed back in six days* from the meridian of Winter Harbour, to the entrance of Sir James Lancaster's Sound, a distance which required *five weeks to traverse*, when going in the opposite direction, seems to afford a *reasonable ground for concluding*, that an attempt for effecting the N.W. passage might be made with a *better* chance of *success from* Behring's Strait, than from the side of America. There are some circumstances, however, which in my opinion render this mode of proceeding altogether *impracticable*, at least for *British* ships. The principal of these arises from the length of the voyage which must first be performed in order to arrive at the point where the work is to be begun. After such a voyage, admitting that no serious wear and tear had been experienced, the most important part of a ship's resources, namely, the *provisions* and *fuel*, must be very materially reduced, and this *without* the *possibility* of renewing them to the extent necessary for such a service, and which can alone give confidence in the performance of an enterprise of which the nature is so precarious and uncertain. Nor should it be forgotten how *injurious* to the health of the crews, so sudden and extreme a change of climate would in all probability prove, as that which they must necessarily experience

Data.   Y

in going at once from the heat of the torrid zone into
the intense cold of a long winter upon the northern
shores of America. Upon the whole, therefore, I cannot but consider, that any expedition equipped by
Great Britain, with this view, will act with greater advantage by at once employing its best energies in the
attempt to penetrate from the eastern coast of America
along its northern shores."

Now, if the practicability of the N.W. passage were
doubted, or its *non*-existence deemed *possible* even, it
appears to me that the *only reasons* why it would be
imprudent to make the attempt *from* Behring's Strait
to the eastward, are the VERY TWO which Captain
Parry, in the first paragraph of the foregoing extract,
says " seem to afford a *reasonable* ground for concluding that an attempt might be made with a *better chance*
of *success from Behring's* Strait than the side of America." Because every seaman ought to know, that in case
of failure in an attempt *from west to east*, by finding *land*,
or the *western* entrances of Straits so encumbered with
ice as to oppose his further advance, he would rather
have a *free wind* to return with, as Captain Parry *had*
when " he sailed back in six days a distance of 600
miles, which required five weeks to traverse," than
these " westerly and north-westerly winds" to *beat* back
against.

As these winds were " always found to produce the
effect of clearing the southern shores of the new Georgian Islands of ice," it may be presumed that they must
also produce the effect of *encumbering* the *northern* and
western shores of islands, as well as the northern and
western entrances of Straits existing between them,
with ice—IF there *be* any to windward. Consequently,
ships proceeding from west to east, and finding such

western entrances closed against them by ice, would
be in a much worse predicament than Captain Parry
was, for instance, when he found the *western* entrance
of the Strait of the Fury and Hecla *actually so closed*
against him by ice. For his obstruction being to *windward* of him, he had only to quit it and return home,
" with these winds from the West and N.W. prevailing"
in his *favor*, and perhaps the " circumvolving current"
of the Quarterly Review into the bargain. Whereas,
any ship having advanced *from* Behring's Straits as far
as the *western* limit of such obstruction as Captain Parry
met with, must have been reduced to the necessity of
beating back again the way she came; unless some
channel could be discovered to the northward, communicating with Barrow's Strait and Lancaster Sound,
which it is hoped Captain Parry will find by way of
Prince Regent's Inlet.

But no such obstruction from ice, and indeed but
little from even land intervening, *can* have entered into
the *calculation* of those who have said, " We *firmly
believe* that a navigable passage *does exist*, and may be
of *no difficult* execution. It is the business of *three
months* out and home. We have little doubt of a *free*
and *practicable* passage for *seven* or *eight* months in
every year. Arrived on the coast of America, and
no obstruction from land occurring, we see NO REASON
why the passage to Icy Cape, which does not exceed
1500 miles, might not *easily* be accomplished in *one
season;* about 600 of these were actually run on the
last voyage in *six days;*" and finally Captain Parry
himself " has recorded his opinion in favor of its accomplishment."

To persons thus sanguine in their hope, nay, so confident in their expectations of success, the prevalence
" of westerly and north-westerly winds" must be, of

all others, the most favorable circumstance, as they would ensure the *speediest* performance of the voyage : for, as " they seem" to Captain Parry, so they do in truth, for *that reason*, " afford a *reasonable* ground" (to them) " for concluding that an attempt might be made with a *better chance* of success *from* Behring's Strait than the side of America." Indeed, as the Quarterly Reviewer sees *no reason* " why the passage to Icy Cape, which does not exceed 1500 miles, may not be *easily* accomplished in *one season*, as 600 of these were actually run in six days, *by means* of these very *westerly* and north-westerly winds," I would take the liberty of asking him, why—(*if* he have no fear of either icy or land impediment) should not the whole 1500 miles be perhaps run with the same facilities in about *one month?* which would be far less than what *he* considers to be the duration of one season, who " has little doubt of a *free* and *navigable* passage for seven or eight months in every year."

The only objections, then, which these advocates for the existence and practicability of a N.W. passage *can* make, consistently with their publicly expressed belief of there being *no obstruction from ice*, and little or none from land, are those given by Captain Parry, in the terms I have quoted ; not one of which appears to me to be of the slightest importance, compared to that which has been given to the discovery of this famed N.W. passage.

And, were it not that *he* has published them, and that therefore, those who know little or nothing of the matter may think them very solid objections, they would hardly deserve the notice of any seaman who has had years of experience on service in ships of war, in all the climates of the globe, except perhaps within the north frigid zone, of whose imaginary inclemency as to the human *feeling*, and its terrible effects, Captain Parry has proved and recorded the *non-existence*, by a practical experience which, being well merited, has been justly rewarded. We will, however, examine them one by one, and see what they amount to.

In the first place, " the length of the voyage to the point where the work is to be begun" is objected to by Captain Parry, and in his opinion renders " this mode of proceeding *altogether impracticable*, at least for *British ships*." But why for " *British* ships" particularly, any more than Russian, or indeed any other ships ? In the present improved state of navigation, the length of the voyage, say first to Macao in China, is absolutely not worthy of a thought. The wear and tear of that part of the voyage might be with ease repaired there or in the Typa. The reduction in the stores, provisions, and fuel, could be made up there just as well as in England ; and if it could not, every thing considered to be absolutely necessary might be sent out and placed there in store preparatory to their arrival. As to the observation, " How *injurious* to the health of the crews, so *sudden* and *extreme* a change of climate would *prove*, as that which they must necessarily experience in going at once from the heat of the torrid zone into the intense cold of a long winter upon the northern shores of America," it must by no means be " necessarily" so, or at all *probable* that the healths of the crews would suffer in the slightest degree, from any changes of climate to which they might be subjected in the course of their voyage. For who that has served (as perhaps Captain Parry *has not*,) during the last war, for years, in all the climates of the globe, and been *as suddenly* removed from hot to cold, and from cold to hot, ever contemplated or experienced any such injurious effects, either upon himself or his ship's companies? None, I dare say; at least I can answer for myself. Many, very many, after being grilled in the East or West Indies for years, immediately on their return home have been sent smoking-hot, to cool in the North Sea in winter, without at all feeling its effects, more than the crews of any other ships long stationed there. But perhaps I shall be told, that the severity of the North Sea climate is *nothing* compared to that of the *terrible* icy regions of the north. Certainly, the North Sea climate may not be so cold ; but its *humidity* renders men much more liable to pulmonary and inflammatory complaints, than it appears Captain Parry's people ever were in the frigid climate of Winter Harbour. For he says, " In the severest weather, not a single inflammatory complaint occurred, though in passing from the cabins into the open air, and *vice versa*, the men were constantly in the habit, for some months, of undergoing a change of from 80 to 100 degrees, and in several instances 120° of temperature." No such extreme change of temperature as this (which, however, had no injurious effect at all,) could *possibly* be experienced on a passage from England to China. There the crews might be refreshed for months, if it were required. From Macao, the passage, with the S.W. Monsoon, could be performed with ease, and in as short a time, to Behring's Strait, as one from England to the N.E. part of America ; so as to be off Icy Cape in all July, if necessary.

So that on every consideration except expense, (which can be nothing with such an IMPORTANT object in view,) certainly, the best and most *expeditious* mode of performing that part of the voyage to the northward of the continent of America, (*if no* obstruction from either land or ice be supposed to exist,) would undoubtedly be, by way of Behring's Strait *to the eastward.* But those who *do* apprehend that obstruction *may* be *probably* met with, somewhere between Behring's Strait and the N.E. part of America, will prudently prefer having the attempt made *from east* to west, but FIRST to *examine* Behring's Strait.

I shall conclude, for the present, with a passage on this subject, written by the late Admiral Burney, and published in the year 1819.

" *Behring's Strait* being regarded as the most probable opening on the western side of America, by many as the only probable one, for the entrance into the Pacific, by a northern navigation from *Europe;* and on the eastern side of America, there being many inlets and arms of the sea unexplored, of which a very small proportion can be expected to lead to *Behring's Strait;* it follows, that the best chance for discovering a passage, or for discovering that there is *no* passage, is by commencing on the other side of America. On this side of America the question can only be set at rest by the discovery of a passage, for twenty expeditions with the most favorable seasons would be insufficient for ascertaining that there is no passage."

If, as the Quarterly Review says, there *be* " a free and navigable passage for seven or eight months in every year," the coast of America must of course form the south side of it. That coast *can* be got hold of at Behring's Strait, and if it *could* be *kept sight* of, and there be *no* obstruction, a ship by tracing it must ultimately discover it : and in less than half the time it can possibly be done from east to west, with the prevailing winds and the Reviewer's circumvolving current against her ; even allowing that she may get at once close in upon the coast of America, by way of Prince Regent's Inlet, or other yet undiscovered channels. But if that inlet fail, "twenty" other expeditions *may* also fail, as Ad‑ miral Burney justly observes, by *as many* channels, if they exist. On the contrary, one attempt from Behring's Strait, whether there be obstruction or not, would per‑ haps decide the question for ever. The most certain mode, however, and doubtless the least expensive, must be by land expeditions ; and if such means had been tried in the year 1818, in all probability it would have been decided by this time.

Though, in this inquiry, I have attempted to show that the Quarterly Reviewer's belief in the practicability and existence of a north-west passage was originally formed on an assumption of circumstances and sup‑ posed facts, as vague, crude, and inconsistent with each other, as they are contrary to the laws of nature, and which even the future proof of *both* cannot establish as *true ;* and though it is tolerably clear, that none of the great *commercial* advantages which his glowing but wild imagination anticipated, can ever be the result of that proof; yet many others undoubtedly have been, and will yet be, obtained by means of the naval expedi‑ tions, and which it is highly to the glory and honor of the first maritime power in the world should have been sent out.

It perhaps would have been better not to have avowed to the world, *at first*, that the grand object of these expeditions was "the discovery of a north-west passage," where success must be so doubtful; but merely to have said, they were fitted out in this "piping time of peace," for the purpose of exploring the Arctic re‑ gions ; to obtain facts, to make observations on their various phænomena, for the extension of science, by throwing light on many subjects as yet but little under‑ stood. In this case all the information they brought

home would have been acceptable to the public from
its novelty, to the philosopher from its value, and clear
gain to all, unalloyed by any feeling of disappointment;
and if the north-west passage should have been *unexpect-
edly discovered*, the gaping world would have considered
it as the *ne plus ultra* of all human enterprise, in short
something like a trip to the moon in a balloon; for,
indeed, the notion which many persons even at present
entertain of it is something like that. The Quarterly
Reviewer, himself, in No. 49, page 214, observes that,
" in proportion as the expectations of the public have
been raised," not so much perhaps, as *he says*, " by the
result of Captain Parry's last Voyage" as by what he
has written, " would a failure be felt. Indeed, we have
no doubt that any thing short of reaching the Pacific
would now be considered as a failure, and cause disappointment, even if it should be discovered that no communication exists between the Atlantic and the Pacific."

Certainly, there can be no doubt but it would *be
a failure;* and though the public in general would consider it such, yet I must confess, as one of that public,
though I should feel great regret, I cannot say I should
be disappointed ; because my expectations have not
been unduly raised, nor shall I ever think that any one
of these expeditions was fitted out in vain. Who, indeed,
can be so narrow-minded as to say, what is the *use* of
all these expeditions ? why all this expense ? except
those who measure the value of every thing by the
commercial scale?

The undertaking is one every way worthy of this
country. The man, whoever he was, who first suggested it, is justly entitled to that praise which every one
of enlarged and liberal mind will award him, whether
it succeed to its full extent or not. Nor will the No-

Data. Z

bleman who presides at the Admiralty fail of that
reward from posterity which he so richly merits, for
having attended to his suggestions, and so far carried
them into effect.

SCRUTATOR.

POSTSCRIPT.

A few days after the foregoing sheets were written, Captain Parry's long-expected "Journal of a Second Voyage for the Discovery of a North-West Passage" made its appearance. After carefully reading it, I cannot say that I have met with a single fact of sufficient weight to induce me to alter one line I had written, or to doubt the correctness of any of the inferences I had drawn from Data previously furnished. On the contrary, I have found much to confirm them. The grand source of the flood-tide in Hudson's Bay is proved to be the Atlantic. It set to the westward generally from Resolution Island all the way to the coast of America, but taking local directions imposed on it by intervening lands. The rate of flow (except in confined channels and inlets) decreased in advancing to the *westward*, as did also the rise and fall of the tide, in proportion to the distances of the places where it was observed from Hudson's and Cumberland Straits, &c.

What I most desired to know, was, whether or not any current had been experienced in the Strait of the Fury and Hecla from the westward.

In the event of there being any such, I presumed to anticipate its effect on floating ice, should there be any, at its western mouth, whatever might be the source or cause of that current; but at the same time denying that the waters of the Pacific Ocean could possibly form any part of it.

Captain Parry did find a current from the westward, running through the Strait of the Fury and Hecla, of which, and the tides in that Strait, he writes thus at page 354 of his Journal : " I believe there can be little doubt that the flood-tide here comes from the westward. That there is, besides this, during a great *part* of the *summer*, a permanent current setting from the same direction, is also sufficiently apparent; and the joint effects of these two causes appear to account satisfactorily for the various irregularities observed, as well in the set of the stream, as in the rise and fall of water by the shore. The natural inference, with respect to the current, seemed at the time to be, that it is *occasioned* by the annual melting of the snows upon the shores of the Polar Sea, for which this Strait affords the only outlet leading to the southward, within perhaps some hundreds of miles; and this supposition appeared the more reasonable from the circumstance of the current having just now [20th September, 1822,] *ceased*, when the streams from the land were once more arrested by the frost of the approaching winter." '

In fact, then, this current was only *periodically* " permanent ;" and, admitting Captain Parry to be correct in his inference as to its cause, it therefore cannot be a part of the Quarterly Reviewer's " circumvolving current from the Pacific through Behring's Strait," which he believes to be " perpetual." For if that circumvolving current of his between the Pacific and Atlantic be perpetual, and there really exist an unobstructed course for it all the way from Behring's Strait, and through that of the Fury and Hecla, as " the only outlet leading to the southward," why should it have " ceased" there about the 20th of September? Captain Parry's own explanation is quite conclusive, that the Reviewer's current can have nothing at all to do with the one he met with in the Strait of the Fury and Hecla. Were this current perpetual, so much the worse. Its *temporary* adverse operation is quite bad enough, for, according to Captain Parry's account of it, it flows eastward, *during* the *only navigable* season, and ceases with it.

The effect of this current is thus described by him at page 489: " The state of the ice for two successive summers, in the Strait of the Fury and Hecla, seems to indicate that the obstruction we there met with, is dependent rather on *locality* than season. It is more than probable, that the obstacles which finally arrested our progress in the Strait, are to be *mainly* attributed to the current we found setting to the eastward through it, and which coincides with that observed by Captain Franklin, and by the Russians, to the westward." True—it does so—as to *direction;* but the *cause* which Captain Parry assigns for its *periodical* flow and *cessation,* renders it *impossible* to *identify this* current with the one they observed, which is said to be perpetual. " This stream," Captain Parry adds, " in finding its way through the Strait, would undoubtedly have the effect of keeping the ice *close home* upon its *western* mouth, so as to prevent the egress of a ship in that direction : and I cannot help thinking that, on that account, the navigation of that Strait will seldom, if ever, be practicable."

On what possible ground, then, can it be expected that the *western* mouth of any other existing Strait between Prince Regent's Inlet and Behring's Strait should, under *similar circumstances,* be more practicable than that of the Fury and Hecla ?

Though Captain Parry says that " circumstances beyond the reach of any previous *speculation,* have combined to oppose an insurmountable barrier to our entrance into the Polar Sea by the route lately pursued," yet *some* of these very circumstances were actually pointed out by the Quarterly Reviewer as the causes of the failure of all former attempts, made in that quarter to discover a north-west passage. Nay—all of these circumstances, as well as the result of Captain Parry's last voyage, were anticipated, and in my hearing mentioned to many private friends by one who deemed the judgment of the Quarterly Reviewer quite sound *only* on *that* point, but who at the same time firmly believed that Repulse Bay had been " satisfactorily examined;" never, like him, having doubted that Middleton was, what Captain Parry has now proved him, a man of veracity.

Captain Parry says, " However unsuccessful have been our late endeavors, they were unquestionably directed to the right place," and that, " with the limited geographical information we then possessed, no other route than that pointed out in my instructions could possibly have been pursued with any reasonable hope of success."

Certainly the route through Hudson's Strait and Bay did, to those who selected it, hold forth more hope at the time than any other, because it was preferred ; and even after failure has proved it to be the *wrong*, it is still proclaimed as the " right place," and as the *only* route that could possibly have been pursued with any reasonable hope of success !

But this necessarily places the route by Prince Regent's Inlet very low indeed in the scale of hope ; for at the time Captain Parry sailed last, that inlet was as well known to him as it is now. No addition has been made to the then limited geographical information he possessed immediately belonging to *itself*. If, then, three years ago, Prince Regent's Inlet were considered, as it is here acknowledged to have been, as *not* holding forth " any reasonable hope of success," on what can a more reasonable hope be built *now*? For my own part, I must confess that I dare not indulge expectation of more from the next attempt through Prince Regent's Inlet, &c. than Captain Parry's strenuous endeavors effected in " the right place ;" and therefore, supported by an acknowledgement from such authority, I still consider it to be what I have already termed it, the FORLORN HOPE. And that too, notwithstanding Captain Parry concludes his Journal in these words, which I sincerely wish may one day prove to be prophetic : " I never felt more sanguine of ultimate success in the enterprise in which I have lately been engaged, than at the present moment ; and I cannot but entertain a confident hope, that England may yet be destined to succeed in an attempt which has for centuries past engaged her attention, and interested the whole civilised world."

THE END.

For EU product safety concerns, contact us at Calle de José Abascal, 56–1°, 28003 Madrid, Spain or eugpsr@cambridge.org.

 www.ingramcontent.com/pod-product-compliance
Ingram Content Group UK Ltd.
Pitfield, Milton Keynes, MK11 3LW, UK
UKHW012344130625
459647UK00009B/507